Praise for *The Enneagram for Black Liberation: Return to Who You Are Beneath the Armor You Carry*

"Chichi Agorom's voice is a part of the reckoning that has been needed in the culture of the Enneagram. Writing with clarity and heart, she describes the map of the Enneagram and the armor that marginalized identities have depended on to survive in a culture of white supremacy and patriarchy. This is simply a great book on the Enneagram and an offering to our collective liberation."

—Renée Rosario, MA, LPC, Core Faculty member of The Narrative Enneagram

"Chichi Agorom is inviting us to center Black women's wholeness in order to define and find "true" liberation that sees us all. She proves, through beautiful storytelling and masterful teaching, that when black women are free we all will be free. This book is pure womanist ethic at work."

—EbonyJanice Moore, hip hop Womanist scholar & founder of Black Girl Mixtape

"This is the most important Enneagram book I have ever read. While this book was written specifically to further the cause of Black liberation, it should be in the hands of every Enneagram enthusiast. By highlighting how our place in society, inherent privilege, and unearned power affect our ability to lay down the armor of our type, Chichi has made the Enneagram and the deep, healing work it invites us into something truly accessible and useful to everyone."

—Abi Robins, author of *The Conscious Enneagram*

"In this book, Chichi Agorom answers the commodified, memeified self-help version of Enneagram with an invitation to become free of entrenched survival patterns, more connected to self and others, and ultimately more whole using this spiritual-emotional tool that can help us truly awaken to who we are meant to be. By centering the experience of Black women, she offers us a path for understanding the Enneagram as a tool for collective liberation."

–Micky ScottBey Jones, The Justice Doula, founder of Enneagram for the People, Certified Enneagram Teacher and Coach

"Chichi Agorom's *The Enneagram For Black Liberation* reclaims seemingly lost identity, reimagines what is possible for Black Bodies, and decolonizes concepts and spaces that refuse to center our experiences. I will be using and recommending this powerful tool of love and liberation throughout my lifetime."

–Thea Monyée, EcoWomanist, Oya Priestess, and Creative Healer

"*The Enneagram for Black Liberation* is a beautiful embrace of the Enneagram system as a tool for freedom and transformation, as well as a powerful critique of ways the Enneagram has been taught through the singular lens of dominant culture, which has limited greater liberation for those with marginalized identities."

– Rev. Dr. Christopher T. Copeland, spiritual director and Core Faculty member of The Narrative Enneagram

THE ENNEAGRAM FOR
BLACK LIBERATION

The ENNEAGRAM for BLACK LIBERATION

Return to Who You Are
Beneath the Armor You Carry

CHICHI AGOROM

BROADLEAF BOOKS
MINNEAPOLIS

THE ENNEAGRAM FOR BLACK LIBERATION
Return to Who You Are Beneath the Armor You Carry

30 29 28 27 26 25 24   1 2 3 4 5 6 7 8 9

Library of Congress Control Number 2024940692 (print)

Cover design: Marcie Lawrence

Hardcover ISBN: 978-1-5064-7896-8
eBook ISBN: 978-1-5064-7897-5
Paperback ISBN: 979-8-8898-3304-8

To my youngest self—the one who always knew she was enough, deserving of love without effort, divine: thank you for showing me the way back home.

CONTENTS

CONTENTS

INTRODUCTION

I am, in addition to many other things, an Enneagram teacher and practitioner because I believe in the power of this tool to help us move toward our more integrated selves. I distinctly remember when I realized that, while I had utilized my type for so many years to navigate the world, I was more than just this type structure that had held me up. This realization gave me so much freedom to explore the fullness of who I am outside of my type.

There are many ways to work with the Enneagram. It can serve as an aid in self-discovery, relational health, organizational development, and so much more. For me, the most profound way that working with the Enneagram has helped my personal growth is as a tool to rediscover who I am separate from who I always believed I needed to be in order to be loved. From my own personal work and from my experience working with many others, I know the Enneagram can help free us from our limiting stories of who we think we must be to be okay and offer us a path to wholeness and freedom. I wrote this book to offer that invitation to you.

In the time I spent training to become an Enneagram teacher and practitioner, I was often the only Black person in the room. The content of the trainings was deep, complex, and nuanced, but to me, it very often seemed privileged. It required a certain level of protection gained from privilege and power to be able to do the work of integration without facing any harm. I started to wonder how these conversations about the Enneagram would shift if the experiences of those who hold marginalized identities were centered. Naming issues around structures of power, systems of oppression, and access to privilege and power within those systems made it clear to me that Enneagram work is not the same for everyone.

When I centered myself in all of my particularities–Black, woman, immigrant–I was able to use the Enneagram in a way that helped me find more freedom. That is why this book centers Black women in our exploration of the Enneagram as a tool for liberation. I believe wholeheartedly that when Black women are free, we will all be free. My hope as an Enneagram teacher is to create more space for Black and Brown bodies within Enneagram learning communities. I hope to teach in a way that honors and centers our lived experiences and acknowledges that different work is required of centered folks than of those whose identities are marginalized. And I want to center our healing, rest, and liberation in a world that demands that we continue to labor and suffer for the advancement of others but never ourselves.

However, even though I intentionally center Black women, this book is for everyone. Liberation is everyone's work, not just the work of those who are harmed by systems of oppression. If your lived experience is different– if your identities are centered or you have more access to power and privilege–I invite you to engage this book with openness, curiosity, and a willingness to investigate what role your own type's armor has played in upholding harmful systems and harmful narratives within yourself.

I believe it is important to know who your teacher's teachers are because it helps ground our study and practice in lineage. Knowing who you are learning from, and who that person learned from, offers not only a sense of greater connection but also a system of accountability. Thousands of Enneagram teachers and coaches exist out there today. In fact, almost anyone can read a couple of books on the Enneagram and begin typing people based on that cursory knowledge. But cursory knowledge severed from its lineage and context can be used in harmful ways, whether intentional or not. We risk using the tool in a misguided way at best or using it to perpetuate harm at worst. For example, using the Enneagram as a way to place people in boxes that restrict the fullness of who they are based on certain characteristics is a misuse of the system and can be harmful.

I studied under the teachers at the Narrative Enneagram (TNE), one of two of the original Enneagram schools in the United States. TNE has been around since 1988, founded by Helen Palmer and David Daniels. Helen Palmer was a student of Claudio Naranjo, who was a student of Oscar Ichazo, who was influenced by the teachings of George Gurdjieff, who was a student of many spiritual traditions across cultures. This is the lineage from which I learned about the Enneagram.

I use the model of the Narrative Tradition in my work with the Enneagram and in my approach to this book. Because there is more than one school of thought around the Enneagram, I think you'll find it helpful to understand the basic framework of the Narrative Tradition and how it guides our exploration of the Enneagram.

TNE teaches the Enneagram through the three branches of psychology, spirituality, and somatics. An integrated life requires balance between awareness, receptivity, and somatics. Through psychology, we begin to name and understand our patterns. Spirituality offers us an invitation to open ourselves up to the possibilities that exist outside of the singular story by which we have lived. And somatic work invites us to be present in our bodies so that we can interrupt these patterns that live in our cells and neural pathways.

Somatic work is incredibly important to working with the Enneagram because our habits and patterns do not simply exist as thoughts. Our bodies enact patterns of behavior that, carried out over time, become unconscious. By unconscious I mean that we don't even have to think about doing things a certain way or reacting a certain way—our bodies simply repeat the pattern for us. So while it is important to be able to cognitively understand the elements of your type structure, for meaningful transformation, you need to work with your body as well.

Another very important element of the Narrative Tradition is storytelling, which is one of the gifts that learning through panels gives us. We know that our brains are wired to create stories as a way to make sense of life and our experiences. We also tend to better connect with and gain a deeper understanding of a concept when we hear it in story form. The same is true for our understanding of type structure and the many ways it plays out. Sharing stories helps us to see the varied ways one type structure can show up in different people's bodies based on their life experiences, families of origin, cultures, and other factors. In keeping with this tradition, stories will be scattered throughout the book, told by Black people who identify with the different types. Some of these stories were shared in a group conversation via Zoom with both old and new friends. Witnessing each person share about the different armor they carry around all the time was a balm in itself. Some of the other stories were sent to me either through voice memos or in written format. I am humbled that these nine people were willing to be vulnerable in sharing about their armor to help illustrate how these themes show up in a real person's life. One story is highlighted per type, and you will find them in boxes throughout the type chapters. While you might not resonate fully with each person's depiction of how the type shows up for them, I hope that as you read their stories, you are able to see some reflections of yourself that help you feel less alone and more known.

For centuries, the Enneagram was handed down by word of mouth in sacred circles, and the Narrative Tradition seeks to continue that legacy through the way we teach the Enneagram. Teaching is done with the aid of panels where people share their own lived experiences of type structure and work with whatever comes up in the moment. The idea here is that there isn't one "expert" in the room who holds all the wisdom. Instead, we bring our collective wisdom to the table and learn from the wisdom that resides in each of our bodies. I often tell Enneagram clients that while I have spent years learning about the system of the Enneagram, I will never know more than they do about their own lived experience of using that type structure to navigate the world. I love the freedom that provides for people to bring their own wisdom to the table. I love the freedom it gives me to be a participant, not an expert, and to trust that there is a collective wisdom that guides us all.

I offer you that same invitation to bring your own wisdom to the table as you read this book. While I have written a book that you have chosen to pick up and read, I am not an expert on your lived experience of being the type you identify with. I offer my wisdom, both inherited and inherent, in these pages. But for you to get the most out of this book, you'll need to bring your own context and lived experience, observe yourself, and listen to your body's wisdom. As we learn to become better observers of ourselves, we create more space within, which allows us to experience freedom.

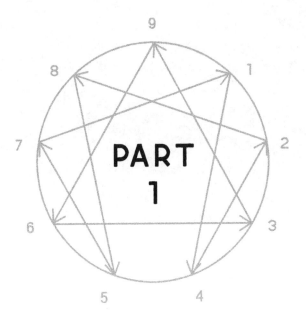

PART
1

Chapter 1
WHY THIS MATTERS

BLACK WOMEN DESERVE TO BE FREE

In the foyer of her mother's church, a dark-skinned, beautiful little girl was surrounded by a small crowd of adults who were all laughing, amused by her three-year-old antics. She was delighted by the attention. It felt natural to be at the center of so much love and joy, without effort. One of the adults—a very tall man—picked her up and tossed her into the air multiple times, a little higher each time. She squealed loudly with each toss and would throw her head back to see just how close to the ceiling she was. Every time his hands left her little body for a few seconds, it felt like she was flying. Beneath her was the crowd of adults who wouldn't let her fall, a circle of smiling faces cheering her on and sharing in her joy. She felt like she could do this forever. Her loud squeals eventually brought out her mother, who was curious to see why her daughter was laughing so hard. Her mother's worry shut down the action quickly. She demanded that no one toss her daughter that high up in the air again. The little girl was immediately returned to the ground and picked up by her mother who hurriedly made her way to the car.

That little girl was me. This is my earliest memory, fuzzy around the edges but one that makes me smile with all my teeth whenever I remember it. For many years I forgot about this version of myself. I still forget her sometimes. When asked about my childhood, the parts that immediately come to mind are the experiences of loneliness, of trauma, of carrying more knowledge of the world's horrors than I should have known at such a tender age. My mother describes it like an on-off switch—one day I was full of joy and laughter, and the next I had withdrawn into myself, quiet and terrified of the world. Those difficult experiences shaped me; they formed the way I showed up in friendships, relationships, and even in my own family.

I grew up too fast, and internally I mourned the loss of a "normal" childhood where I could just be a little girl with no cares in the world. Externally, adults praised me for being so mature for my age. I wasn't a child who showed her anger on the surface, but I felt red-hot rage every time an adult congratulated me for wearing my pain well instead of offering to help remove the heavy burden that wasn't mine to carry in the first place. I would come home and complain to my mother about how much I hated being called mature, and she would laugh, perplexed by why I was so offended by a compliment. I didn't have the language then to explain to her why it hurt so much. Even as an adult, I still feel a less intense version of that rage when I am praised for being "so strong and brave." In my head, I am often yelling at the person complimenting me: *"I don't want to be strong. I don't want to be wise beyond my years. I want the freedom to be soft without fear."*

But being seen as mature or wise had its gifts too. It gave me a role to play in relationships that offered something of value. I could offer the wisdom from the lessons I had learned while keeping my own vulnerability around the pain safely tucked away inside of me. Being seen as brave or strong meant I got a level of respect not offered to those who were perceived as fragile or weak. I had been criticized so often as a child for being too sensitive, so being praised as strong felt like I had successfully fooled everyone into seeing only the parts of me I allowed them to see. No one needed to know how much everything actually affected me, how badly I wanted to feel loved without effort. The risk of pain was too great after all I had experienced, so I used what came naturally to me to try and earn love. Maybe if I was the bravest, wisest, most mature person in a room I would be worthy again of the attention, love, and joy that my three-year-old self received without effort.

I learned how to be "vulnerable" with people without really letting them see me. A part of me was always withdrawn as a mechanism of protection. "You can only hurt the parts of me I give you, and if I never give you all of me, some part of me will remain safe from pain." From my withdrawn vantage point, I would observe people and their behavior. Because my family generally didn't speak much around their experiences of pain, I learned to observe patterns, looking for what people *weren't* saying underneath the many or few words they chose. I wanted to understand why people acted the way they did because it might help me understand why I had ended up the recipient of so much pain. Maybe it would help me understand what to do with the hurt, since it was unacceptable in my Nigerian culture to speak of your pain. Why did other people seem happier than me and my family members? Were they really happy, or was everyone carrying unspoken hurt around with them all the time too? If so, how would we all heal? Did we have to carry around the heavy backpacks filled with pain and suffering and trauma forever?

These questions led me to a master's program in clinical mental health counseling at the age of twenty-four. I finally had the time and resources to live in the space of these questions and gain a better understanding of what motivates our behaviors, how our attachments shape us, how we become resilient, and how we heal. It was during my master's program that I was first introduced to the Enneagram. At the time, I was a bit skeptical of the idea that all of human experience could be divided into nine types. Additionally, the person who introduced the Enneagram to me wasn't someone whose suggestions I deemed trustworthy, so I tossed it out and forgot about it.

But over the next couple of years and through the end of my graduate degree, the Enneagram kept popping up everywhere for me. More and more people I respected were talking about it, and I was beginning to get curious about a system that seemed more dynamic and nuanced than other personality tests I had used up until that point.

The system of the Enneagram invited me to, for the first time, see how much of my energy went into creating an image that was separate from my truest self, what the Enneagram calls the essential self. Without shame, I was given language for the patterns I had noticed over the years, patterns I had come to think of as "just who I am." I began to see how I had wielded the particular behaviors that gained me applause and acceptance into a kind of armor to keep myself safe from pain. The more I understood about my type as armor, the freer I felt to choose when to pick up and put down the armor without confusing it with my true identity.

The kindest gift the Enneagram has given me is a deepened compassion for myself and for others. Its invitation to notice my patterns without judgment and to allow myself to be exactly where I am was transformative for me. I had grown up with the belief that I needed to become a perfect future version of myself in order to be worthy of love, and the Enneagram taught me how to compassionately question that compelling yet untrue story about my lovability. I always felt like an anomaly within my family, my Nigerian culture, and the white American culture I was thrust into at the age of seventeen, so to discover a system that read me *so* perfectly felt like a relief. It wasn't just me after all. As I continued to work with it, I found the permission to be present with my goodness, worthiness, and lovability in each moment. I embrace my humanity more now than I did before I began working with this transformative system.

Once I completed my master's program, I began my training with the Narrative Enneagram to become a certified teacher and practitioner. The first return of that memory of three-year-old me being thrown in the air happened during a visualization exercise at an Enneagram training. My three-year-old self came back to me as an invitation, a reminder of what was true before the pain of the world clouded my ability to see it.

All of my life so far has been a journey to return to the freedom and joy of that little girl who knew she was deserving of love without effort. Those things I believed I had to be to survive are things that are actually true of me. I *am* brave. I *am* wise. I *am* strong. But what I have learned and continue to learn is that my bravery and wisdom aren't what earn me love, belonging, or safety. The danger lies in confusing my strengths with my worthiness. When I do that, I abandon the other parts of myself that I'm convinced make me less worthy. In reality, I am worthy of love when I am doing absolutely nothing, when I am at rest, when I allow myself to be soft, when I am vulnerable, when I make mistakes or am anxious, angry, or sad.

The more space I create between my essential self and the things I learned to do to survive, the closer I feel to three-year-old me. Her freedom and joy don't feel naive; after all, the world was still inequitable and unjust while she soared in the air protected by the circle of love beneath her. Her embodied freedom wasn't grounded in the existence of a perfect world. My three-year-old self—a depiction of my truest self—reminds me that it is possible to embody freedom as a dark-skinned Black immigrant woman while so much pain still exists in an imperfect world.

Because of the way our world is set up, this sounds like a revolutionary concept. Blackness, whether on the continent of Africa or in the diaspora, is often associated with possessing superhuman strength, toughness, and a constant striving to prove we are not who the systems of supremacy tell us we are. Even when we attain success as defined by the systems of supremacy (material wealth, career recognition, fame, etc.), we still can't shake the feelings of not-enoughness. We use protective armor—humor, hardness, or even lighter skin—to get further up the ladder of supremacy rather than in the pursuit of freedom.

On the other hand, sometimes even our work to dismantle systems of oppression can become the altar on which we place our worthiness, believing we are more worthy *because* we are fighting against oppression. Our activism can become another armor we carry that doesn't lend itself to our true freedom and rest. But there is a difference between fighting to *prove* we are worthy and fighting to create a new world *because* we know we are worthy of it. When our fight is grounded in a belief in our inherent worth and dignity, we don't have to carry the fight with us everywhere like armor. We are not here to just fight and suffer until we die. We get to choose rest, ease, and joy for ourselves. We deserve that even while the world is still a raging dumpster fire. We deserve that even while we work toward uprooting the lies of supremacy within us and around us.

We deserve that simply because joy is our birthright. Rest is our birthright.

This book explores the Enneagram as armor that we wield to protect ourselves from pain and offers practices to help create more space between what we do to survive and who we are. This book is also a love letter to Black women in particular. Zora Neale Hurston wrote way back in 1937 that the Black woman is the mule of the world, and those words still ring true in 2021. Black women are often at the forefront of liberatory movements because if we don't fight for ourselves, no one else will. And in the fight for our own liberation, we end up fighting for everyone else's *even when they don't show up for us.* We are dismissed as angry when we demand for people to do better. We are glorified for how well we suffer and applauded by the people who benefit daily from the systems that cause our suffering. We internalize the messages of those systems and punish ourselves for being too much and not enough at the same time. It is exhausting. We most certainly need armor to protect ourselves from the cruelty of this world, but we cannot forget that our armor is only a one-sided story of who we are. We need spaces, both internal and external, where we can exist without the armor.

So, dear Black woman, I hope this book helps you create more space within yourself to embrace all of your complexities—your tenderness and your fire, your hope and your grief, your loudness and your softness, your strengths and your insecurities. You get to be fully human, fully worthy, fully free outside of the white gaze. Each time we come home to our identity beyond survival, it is a taste of freedom. May the taste of freedom linger on our tongues, reminding us what it is we are actually fighting for.

A COLLECTIVE APPROACH TO WHOLENESS WORK

A popular quote, which is frequently cited as an African proverb, says, "If you want to go fast, go alone; if you want to go far, go together." Here in the United States, we live in a go-fast-alone society. And even though I grew up in a collectivist culture that emphasized the go-together lifestyle, my natural tendency is to go fast alone. I'd much rather do something myself than try to figure out the expectations of a whole group of people. The me-centric individualism that is prevalent in the United States makes it easy to believe that an individual's wellness, or lack thereof, is made possible strictly by each person's independent effort. The pick-your-self-up-by-the-bootstraps mentality is a perfect example of this way of thinking, placing both glory and shame on the individual for what they achieve or fail to achieve while ignoring the systems set up for the benefit of only a few.

What we know to be true, however, is that our wellness and liberation do not exist separate from the collective. It is important to be clear, though, about what the word *wellness* means here. Wellness is a state of balance that comes from having our personal, relational, and collective needs met. Because wellness includes the personal, relational, and collective, there can be no wellness without justice. If the systems that govern our communities are structured in a way that ignores or even exacerbates our needs, we cannot be truly well. Those who have the power to protect themselves from systemic harm tend to define wellness simply as "love and light" or "choosing positivity and transcending pain." But how can those who are consistently harmed by these systems ever be well by that definition?

Wellness work is not just the navel-gazing, self-care trend of long baths, face masks, and yoga studio memberships that's been popularized by social media. This insular focus excludes the fact that wellness is our collective responsibility. Wellness and justice work must go hand-in-hand if we are truly to create a more equitable world.

In my post-master's marriage and family therapy program, we talked often about what wellness and healing look like for individuals in the context of the systems in which they exist. For example, someone might come to therapy seeking support for their experience of anxiety. Looking through a purely individualistic lens, the focus of therapy would be to teach the client techniques to soothe or overcome their anxiety. The client might be encouraged to move their body or practice mindful breathing or make lists that help them focus only on what they can control.

If we looked at this same client through a systemic lens, we would become more curious about their identities and how those identities have impacted their history and current lived experience. What is their family system like? Do they feel supported and safe in their everyday life? Are they financially stable? Do they hold a marginalized identity, and if so, how have they experienced harm as a result? Do they have relationships in which they can fully be themselves without fear of harm or retribution?

Let's say the client mentioned above is experiencing anxiety because they are highly qualified but keep being rejected from jobs due to the color of their skin. This leaves them vulnerable to the threat of eviction in the near future. Maybe they also take care of their aging parents financially, and without a steady, well-paying job, their family members will suffer too. While a reminder to move their body and deepen their breath is helpful, it doesn't address the systemic harm at the root of this client's anxiety. Supporting this person's well-being includes not just individual soothing practices but also helping them find resources for the very real threat to their safety. Supporting them might also include holding a safe space for them to name and unlearn the racial gaslighting that often occurs in situations like these, where people of color are held individually responsible for the failings of an entire system.

The work of healing and coming home to our truest selves is deeply personal, but it cannot be extricated from our collective healing. The pursuit of our own healing and freedom has the power to transform our communities and the world. The freer we become on an individual, cellular level, the more freedom we bring to our relationships, our families, our neighborhoods, our communities. In relational community we learn what it is to love and be loved, to hold and be held, to see and be seen. A person who is living from a place of greater freedom has access to more choice—the choice to opt out and not collude with systems that oppress them or to reenact that oppression on others. For example, if we view capitalism as an oppressive system that slowly erodes our humanity as it turns us into machinery for the sake of profit, then a person who becomes freer from the systems of capitalism will have more capacity in their day-to-day life to simply be without producing. And when they can just be, they are able to bring their full attention to the present moment—fully experiencing themselves and the ones around them rather than seeing them as a means to an end. The people around them who get the gift of their full presence are also given permission to show up as fully human in their own circles, thus widening the impact of this freedom.

For meaningful transformation to occur—which is the actual purpose of the Enneagram—we must be willing to divest from the systems that teach us that our "best lives" are all about us and somehow separate from the well-being of the people around us. It is important to shift our conversations about the Enneagram from just the individual to include the whole in which we are held. Even the visual map of the Enneagram is a circle in which all the numbers are held. Not a single one of us exists in a vacuum where our patterns of belief and behavior do not impact others around us. Our wellness and freedom are interconnected, and as we do our individual work to get free, we use our ever-expanding freedom to free others. As Toni Morrison taught us, "the function of freedom is to free somebody else."

Because we live in capitalist and individualist systems, in some Enneagram spaces people are only interested in using the knowledge of their Enneagram type to find the right color palette for their homes or the right diets, exercise routines, or romantic partners. Sometimes, the Enneagram can also be used as a means to climb to the top of the ladder of oppression. We might work hard to create "better" versions of ourselves to earn validation and worth in the eyes of the system without ever really being free.

In the introduction to her book *The Spiritual Dimension of the Enneagram,* Sandra Maitri describes our Enneagram types as a prison from which we are invited into freedom. Unfortunately, some of us learn how to make our prison cells shine and sparkle enough to garner praise while we still remain trapped. Spending our energy trying to be better versions of our types is not the same as getting free.

The United States is referred to as an Enneagram Type Three culture, meaning there is generally a widely held subconscious belief that to be valuable and lovable, you must be seen as successful and capable. In the same way that polishing your prison cell doesn't make you free, working incessantly to achieve success *in order to feel valuable and lovable* doesn't make you free either. Realizing that you have always been and will always be valuable and worthy of love even if you fail at everything you attempt to do is what frees you. It frees you to work hard for what is important rather than for what is required to be seen as successful. It frees you to be yourself rather than perform for applause.

I hope that one of the biggest lessons you take away from this book is that the Enneagram is not just a system that helps the individual reach wholeness and freedom but one that, when held differently, moves us all toward collective freedom, wholeness, and liberation. As we do the work of remembering and returning to the fullness of who we have always been before systems of supremacy forced us to forget, we find rest from the pressures to prove our worthiness, our brilliance, our dignity. We are free to embody rest and ease as our birthright because we're not expending energy trying to prove our worth to systems that thrive on our degradation.

One of my Enneagram teachers, Renée Rosario, once made a powerful statement that has stayed with me for years. She said, "the [Enneagram] type structure *needs* to be seen; wholeness does not need to be seen." In other words, something that is true about you (your inherent worth, for example) will always be true about you, even if no one is there to witness it. And if you actually believe it to be true, all the way down to your bones, you will not need to fight to prove it to the external world. Instead, you will experience the freedom of getting to rest in what is true of you—your worthiness—regardless of the opinions or expectations of the world outside of you.

That is one way to describe my personal journey with the Enneagram as a tool for liberation. And that is what I hope to invite you into in the following chapters. As Tricia Hersey, our collective Nap Bishop, reminds us often: survival is not the end goal for liberation. We must thrive. We will rest.

A NOTE ON LANGUAGE

Language is a malleable thing that evolves with time. With new lived experiences come new words, or the retiring of older words that are no longer accurate or inclusive. In this particular moment in time, there is much attention paid to language—how we name things and one another, and what words best honor the complexities of the human experience.

Language will continue to evolve past the publication of this book, and at some point in the future, the words I use in here might mean something completely different. Some of these words right now already hold different meanings based on the contexts in which they are used. With that in mind, I wanted to be clear about what these words mean to me in the context of this book.

Systems of oppression refers particularly to the systems of white supremacy, capitalism, and patriarchy. We are all born into systems we didn't choose. These systems work well for some at the expense of others. I refer to people that the systems uplift and protect as **centered**. In the United States, those who are centered tend to be white, male, cisgender, heterosexual, Christian, English-speaking, formally educated, able-bodied, wealthy, and slim bodied. People with these identities have access to more unearned power and privilege by virtue of these characteristics.

Those who hold **marginalized identities** in our society are people living in Black, Brown, and Indigenous bodies, women, femmes, trans folk, nonbinary folk, queer folk, people living with disabilities, people living in large bodies, people without formal higher education, non-English speakers, certain immigrants, and people living in poverty. Even though it requires more words, I prefer to use the phrase *people who hold marginalized identities* rather than marginalized people. I do not think of myself as living on the margins; that is a designation made by the systems outside of myself. In my life and in the choices I make, however, I center myself and my well-being.

It is, of course, possible for one person to hold identities that fall into these two categories. Identifying as a cisgender, heterosexual, able-bodied, and formally educated woman gives me access to more privilege than someone who identifies differently in those categories. And yet my dark skin places me on a lower rung of the ladder of white supremacy than a person who holds those same exact identities and lives in a white body. Men are centered even in communities of color, therefore my identity as a woman is still less protected by the system. These **intersectional** identities are important to keep in mind when we explore the relationship between power and vulnerability in chapter 3.

I use **liberation** in this context to mean ending all forms of oppression for all people. It is a worthy cause to fight for, and I believe that we can embody rest, freedom, and ease even now while the fight toward liberation continues. Part of liberation work is freeing ourselves from our internalized oppressions, or the ways in which we have learned to become our own internal oppressors. Also, it is easy to forget that we are more than just the fight or the struggle.

Embodying liberation reminds us that we deserve freedom and rest right now, not just when the battle is won.

Lastly, I refer to **the Enneagram as a tool**, one of *many* tools, that can help us remember who we are and find freedom in returning home to our inherent worthiness, dignity, and power. Because the system of the Enneagram isn't the only tool, you are free to take what works for you and leave the rest. If it is helpful, use it. If it isn't helpful, leave it. Understanding the Enneagram is not an end in itself. If it is not helping you become freer, more awake and more compassionate, it's a good idea to evaluate how you are holding and using this tool.

You can return to this section as you make your way through the rest of the book, as a way to remember and get grounded again in the core of what it is we are exploring.

Chapter 2
THE ENNEAGRAM AS ARMOR

TYPE STRUCTURE AS ARMOR

The Enneagram is a system of human development that teaches us how to work with both the shadow and light within ourselves as we move toward transformation. It gives us a profound map to understand and navigate the complexities of human motivations, and it offers a system in which all those complexities belong. The Enneagram also teaches us how to integrate head, heart, and body in order to live more consciously. It shows us the limiting stories that keep us stuck in our unhelpful patterns and invites us into more expansive stories.

According to the Enneagram, there are nine different ways of being in the world or nine distinct archetypes of personality. We all spend most of our lives utilizing one of these archetypes for survival and satisfaction. On an intrinsic human level, we are motivated to avoid pain and seek pleasure. We want safety, belonging, love, and we find pleasure in experiencing life as safe, offering us love and inherent belonging. But pain is an inevitable part of the human experience, and it shows up in some form during

21

our formative years—whether from rejection, shame, disconnection, or something else. This pain introduces the notion that our access to safety, belonging, and love might not always be secure.

Our brains, which are wired for survival, then work hard to ensure that we are protected from that particular kind of pain reoccurring. We subconsciously begin to act in a way that protects us from that painful experience being repeated. The longer we do this, the more these actions become embedded in our bodies as habitual patterns of responding to the world. Those patterns become what we refer to as our personalities or our ego structures, and most of us tend to confuse our personalities with our essence—our true selves. But the Enneagram invites us to consider that the patterns we have utilized to avoid pain might not actually be the fullness of who we are. By helping us see and name these patterns, the Enneagram offers us a map to return to who we truly are outside of them.

So if our type structures form with the primary goal of helping us avoid pain and orienting us toward pleasure (and pleasure is defined or experienced differently by each type), we could think of them as armor. Armor serves primarily to protect us from threats, like the hard shell of a turtle or a snail. These animals carry around their protective shells with them wherever they go, and these shells are useful in keeping them protected from the threats of the world around them. The armor is a part of them, but it's not the entirety of who they are. They can disappear behind their shells when they feel threatened and reemerge when they feel safe.

Similarly, our types offer a protective layer from the particular fears we have. Our types work hard to protect us from the pain and suffering an imperfect world brings us by keeping our soft, vulnerable selves hidden. They exist to protect us from further harm and to acquire for us a certain form of love, security, and belonging. But the kind of love, security, and belonging our types get for us, in some ways, is an imitation. This is because our types tell a singular story about who we must be in order to access love, security, and belonging. Anything about us that doesn't fit into that singular story is dismissed, ignored, or avoided as a threat to our love, security, and belonging. We begin to really believe this singular story that says we must be just one thing in order to have what we desire.

These stories help us make sense of the world in a binary, either-or way. For example, as children we saw our parents as all-knowing and all-powerful. They were bigger than us, smarter than us, and seemed to have eyes behind their heads that caught us the instant we tried to mess around. We experienced ourselves as the center of their worlds—or at least we expected to be at the center of their worlds. We might have seen them as the architects of our overall childhood experiences, whether good or bad. As we get older, this singular view widens into a more complex, nuanced understanding that allows us to see our parents as humans who are imperfect and who had their own struggles that had nothing to do with us! In this expansive view, we can hold multiple things as true rather than subjecting our parents to the singular view that we held as children. In the same way, working with the Enneagram invites us into a more expansive story. We are offered a mirror that reflects back to us the singular, constricting story we have believed about ourselves so that, if we choose, we can access a fuller, more expansive story. Ultimately, a continued practice with the Enneagram helps us experience more freedom and more choice in our experience of self, others, and the world. We get to experience the depth and breadth of the love, security, and belonging that is inherently ours, with no need to earn, control, or prove anything.

One of the biggest differences between the Enneagram and other personality typing tools is the fact that the focus of the Enneagram is less on behavior and more on core motivations—our deepest needs, desires, and wounds. For example, you and I could appear really similar on the surface, maybe both interested in drawing and painting during our free time. Art for you might be a way to practice allowing yourself to get comfortable with imperfection, learning to accept whatever comes out onto the paper without criticism. For me, it is about taking the jumbled thoughts and emotions inside of me and working with them until they make sense outside of me. It is a way to sort through the murky waters of my internal world and create something cohesive and beautiful from it. We might both create pieces of art that look similar, but our core motivations are vastly different.

The thing with core motivations is that we cannot tell what a person's core motivation is based solely on their behavior. As we saw in the example above, there is so much more at work beneath the decision to pick up a pencil or paintbrush than what is usually immediately obvious on the surface.

Our type structures hold many gifts and are incredibly useful in navigating our interpersonal relationships. They help us understand what motivates us, and they offer us a particular view of reality that is necessary, useful, and beautiful. Our work isn't to get rid of our types or distance ourselves from them. If we do so, we miss out on their particular gifts. Our work is to create space between who we are and the armor we carry so that within that space we can find freedom, choice, and expansion. Most of us carry around our armor for so long that we begin to confuse who we are with the things we do to survive. But we are not our types; we utilize our types to help us navigate the pain that exists in our world and in our stories. The Enneagram invites us to recognize that we are the people behind the armor, not simply the armor itself.

THE ESSENTIAL SELF

The system of the Enneagram teaches us that we each have a true self—what we call an essential self—in addition to our personality structures, which we call our types. Our essential selves are who we have always been, the purest, truest essence of being that we were when we entered this world. I think of our essential selves as who we were before the pains of life touched us. Like me and my three-year-old self, if you have memories that go back to when you were little, you might be able to recall the body memory of what it was like to be free to experience love, safety, and belonging without effort. Toddlers are such a pure depiction of this essential nature. They experience every new thing with delight and curiosity. They don't hide when they're in pain—they express it and ask for soothing. They know that they are deserving of love and attention, and they ask for it often and without shame. Think of how little kids ask you to watch them dance or to watch how fast they can run or how high they can jump. They are delighted with themselves, and they want you to join in that delight. When you join their delight, you find that you can access that space within yourself too—that playful, joyful, peaceful place that allows you to delight in the world around you and let yourself be delighted in.

This essential nature never goes away as we get older. We just lose contact with it, and without a conscious practice to return home to it, we forget what it's like to be that free. Our minds might forget, but our bodies hold memories of our essential natures, and working with our bodies can help us reconnect to our essence. Our essential selves are connected to the objective reality that is expansive, rich, and multidimensional. This objective reality is where we experience the Holy Ideas of our types. The Holy Ideas are nine different perspectives on reality that are not filtered through the lens of personality. Each type is sensitive to a particular one of these Holy Ideas, and it is that Holy Idea they lose contact with when they begin to see the filter of their personality as the ultimate reality. The Holy Ideas aren't fixed or static states of consciousness but more expansive and fluid experiences of reality. In other words, the Holy Ideas—and our essential selves—usher us into reality as it is, while our types create a subjective filter that we mistake for the fullness of reality. We will explore the Holy Idea of each type in part 2.

The invitation in our work with the Enneagram is to make a practice of reconnecting to the essential nature, to the true self that exists underneath our armor and underneath our woundedness. When we can do this, we can experience freedom, joy, rest, and ease that isn't predicated on our environment. In a world that is often unsafe, especially for those who hold marginalized identities, this practice of rediscovering home within ourselves reminds us that our bodies can be a resource of safety and love no matter what the outside world throws at us. When I forget this truth, I start to experience my body as a repository for pain and trauma and anxiety and heartache. But in reality, my body is also a home for joy, ease, love, connection, safety, and belonging. Creating space between my true self and the armor I have carried has allowed me more access to my own essential nature. That space is what I hope to invite you into throughout this book.

THE POWER OF SPACE

In one of my favorite quotes, which is often used to describe the life of Viktor Frankl, Stephen R. Covey paraphrases, "Between stimulus and response, there is a space. In that space is our power to choose our response. In our response lies our growth and our freedom."

We forget the space all the time. Our type structures respond with immediacy to anything they perceive as a threat to their security, love, and worth. In the white-centric culture of our Western society, much emphasis is placed on mental intelligence as the most powerful form of knowing. Interestingly, what science teaches us is that our bodies are actually the seat of much of our knowing. What this means when we are talking about the Enneagram is that our patterns and habits don't exist just in our minds. Our patterns are stored and exhibited in our bodies. You don't just *think* yourself into acting like your type; your body responds to external stimuli based on patterns it has built over time while your head creates a story that helps you make sense of, and think you are in control of, your automatic response. Our bodies are where we tense up, contract, jump into action, freeze in inaction. Our types operate with lightning speed without giving us much of a chance to pause and notice what is happening within our bodies. And yet, the particular practice of pausing to notice the space, to *be* in the space, gives us choice and, in that choice, freedom.

It is possible to collect a lot of information about the Enneagram and your type in particular, but without noticing the way those patterns operate in your body, you are simply walking around with a head full of information and no real movement toward transformation. A lot of us enjoy learning about ourselves, connecting the dots around behavior, and gaining new language for things we hadn't previously been able to describe. But there is a difference between information and knowledge. Information offers us facts about a certain thing, while knowledge utilizes both facts and experience. In other words, knowledge requires us to shift from just a collection of facts about type into the actual experiencing of our patterns in motion. What we gain from this is wisdom, and wisdom requires a conscious integration of our heads, hearts, and bodies.

To be able to consciously create space within ourselves in order to exercise choice, we must develop the ability to observe ourselves. We need to be able to practice noticing our patterns without judgment or shame. Think of it this way: Imagine you've fallen asleep in the passenger seat of a car on a long journey. When you begin to wake up, you realize that someone else has been making the calls about how fast or slow to go, where to turn, what is considered an incoming threat and how to respond to it. You've been along for the ride, but without any control of the process. It is natural to feel upset about the choices that were made on your behalf while you were asleep. It is normal to want to wrestle the driver for control over the car and course correct immediately.

But what if you first simply noticed without shame or judgment? What if you offered gratitude and appreciation to the driver for navigating during all the hours you were asleep? Even if you don't like some of the decisions the driver made, you are still alive, and the car is still in motion. Now that you are awake, you can make more intentional choices about where you're headed and how. You can switch shifts and take over from the driver, knowing that this process will happen over and over again as you work on staying awake or waking up faster when you've fallen asleep.

In this image, the driver is type structure, as you probably already deduced. Our work as sleepy passengers is to become more conscious and awake. To become more conscious and awake, it is essential to build awareness of what it feels like in your body when your armor is on and when it isn't. Your ongoing practice is to first notice what is happening in the moment, bringing your attention to where you feel constriction, tightness, heaviness, a buzzy sensation, etc. Then you pause to slow down the rapid firing of your patterns. You do this by following your breath—paying attention to your inhales and exhales, the way your body expands and contracts with each breath in and out. As you create this pause, you are also allowing the reaction your body is having to simply be there.

Type structures want to swing into action immediately to minimize the threat or distract from the discomfort. But when you notice that happening, pausing and giving space allows you to be present with what is happening. Doing that slows down the rapid-fire impulse and shows you that another way is possible. It is possible to be with the discomfort, the pain, the fear without becoming overwhelmed by or lost in it. That is the power of the space.

Your guides for this ongoing practice are compassion, gratitude, and curiosity. First, compassion invites us to embrace our own humanity with kindness and softness.

THE ENNEAGRAM AS ARMOR

Being human is hard, and it takes work. In nine different ways, our types want to create a rigid and inflexible version of being human that is less about being whole and more about avoiding the vulnerability of discomfort, mistakes, our neediness, failure, abandonment, depletion, helplessness, and deprivation. When we are able to be compassionate with ourselves, we create more space within us to show up as fully human. When we can show up as fully human, we experience freedom. We often shame ourselves and one another for being human, but shame never motivates us to grow. Instead, it keeps us stuck in a cycle of feeling bad about who we are and helpless to change it. Compassion as a guide enables us to be with ourselves exactly as we are in this present moment. We experience transformation when we can be fully present with the parts of us that we tend to run from or avoid.

Gratitude is the second guide to this practice. Gratitude reminds us to see the ways our type structures have worked so hard to keep us safe and help us navigate an imperfect world. Our types aren't the enemy or something that we need to overcome or get rid of. They are a one-sided story attempting to make sense of a multifaceted world, yes, but they have been useful in protecting us. Gratitude reminds us to say thank you. Even as we do the work to become more fully who we are, we can still offer gratitude to the structures that have sustained us thus far. We can also offer gratitude to ourselves for showing up for the hard work of being present. It's easier to just run on autopilot, so remember to thank yourself for showing up for you.

The final guide is curiosity. As we notice, pause, and allow, we also need to practice curiosity about what we are observing. Curiosity paired with compassion and gratitude allows us to ask ourselves, *"What is this feeling connected to? Why is this thought here? When have I felt this way before?"* Compassionate curiosity allows us to discover the truth about our reactions without judgment or shame. When we are able to identify what is really going on, we then have the power to choose how we want to respond. We are no longer on autopilot but are conscious, awake, and living fully in our experience with the freedom to choose how we want to show up.

So, your practice is to notice–pause–allow, and your guides for this practice are compassion, gratitude, and curiosity. The goal of this practice isn't to arrive at a perfectly enlightened future version of yourself. The goal isn't perfection; perfection is an enemy of liberation. This practice is a lifelong commitment to becoming more present, more conscious, more awake, more free. The more we embody this practice, the more space we create between ourselves and our armor. Within that space, we experience the freedom of choice. That is our goal.

As you can see, this work is about *you*. The noticing, the pausing, the allowing–all of that is about your own internal work. Knowledge of this system is not intended for you to use to tell other people who they are and where they need to grow. Focus on your own reactivity; focus on your own growth. As you become more of who you are, which is to say more human, your way of being will be an invitation to others to become more human too.

The Enneagram is not an icebreaker game or a party trick to show off how well you know the [stereo]types and feel powerful as you put people in boxes. All of us are scared of pain and want security, love, and belonging. Just because the eight other types wear their armor differently doesn't mean their ways of being are invalid. Compassion helps us make more room for one another to breathe, to rest, to set down our armor, to practice being in reality without judgment.

When you notice judgment and criticism arise inside of you while you read about various type structures, pause. Take a deep breath and notice what is coming up for you. Maybe the section you're reading reminds you of someone who frustrates you or who hurt you in the past. Instead of going into judgment, offer compassion to your own experience of pain or frustration. Be with it gently; ask it what it needs to feel soothed. Don't give in to the temptation to make it about the other person. We cannot transform other people or force them into wanting transformation. We can only be present within ourselves, notice our own reactions, and consciously choose how to respond in a way that moves us toward transformation.

BODIES AND TRAUMA

While we might think of trauma as something horrific happening to a person, like an assault of some kind, trauma is not actually the event that occurs. Trauma is our body's protective response to the event if it is perceived as dangerous. Trauma always happens in our bodies. For those of us who have experienced trauma, being in our bodies can often feel overwhelming and unsafe. Without adequate resourcing, it is possible to activate our fight-or-flight-or-freeze response when we are attempting to work with our bodies. Learning how to access and experience safety in our bodies is often slow work, meaning it takes time, patience, and compassion. My suggestion for you is to take it slow and get support. Give yourself and your body time and support from people in your life who are good at holding space and asking good questions. If you are able, use a therapist as a resource. This isn't the wholeness Olympics, and there is no medal for who gets freest fastest. Sometimes, part of the work is taking a break, walking away, and taking your focus off of growth work for a while.

In addition to our individual experiences of trauma, the systems of oppression in which we reside also cause trauma responses in our bodies on a regular basis. These systems pose a threat to the safety of many bodies. Every body, even a centered one, is affected adversely by white supremacy and capitalism. However, marginalized bodies in particular experience more of a conscious ongoing threat to their safety and survival. To find safety within these systems, we often have to shift parts of ourselves in order to experience less harm. Whether that is performing for the white gaze, for example, or buying into the allure of money as a source of safety, we subconsciously do what we must in order to survive. The threat to safety is ongoing and repetitive for Black bodies in the United States. Before there is a chance to repair and heal, another threat is presented.

Think about the way your body responds when the news breaks of yet another Black life taken unjustly. Your body might get really tight and be unable to find calm; you might feel on edge or feel the red-hot heat of rage. You might find it difficult to take a full breath. You might cry, yell, or want to hit something. You might feel nothing at all, numb from the overwhelming nature of the trigger. All these, and more, are trauma responses to the constant danger Black bodies are exposed to.

I am writing this chapter a few weeks before the end of 2020, the year in which thousands of people took to the streets in protest following the live video coverage of George Floyd's murder by the police. I wasn't done processing the murders of Ahmaud Arbery and Breonna Taylor before there was yet another, and this time the entire eight minutes and forty-six seconds of horror was filmed live. I chose not to watch the video because my body's trauma response was already in full swing. It took a series of mental gymnastics and deep breathing to get myself to go on a walk in my predominantly white neighborhood for weeks afterward. While I would walk with earphones in, I often had the music turned off. I was hyperaware of my environment, prepared to become the next target of fear and hate. My body was rigid and tight as I walked, the opposite of a free, casual stroll. Complex trauma describes what many Black bodies endure on an ongoing basis.

It can feel overwhelming and stressful to be present in our bodies if we have more practice escaping our bodies than being present with them. Again, my suggestion is to take it slow. In our capitalist society, achieving quick results and quick turnarounds becomes the goal even with our healing work. We want a drive-through or vending-machine approach to unpacking our patterns and finding healing and freedom. That doesn't work here, and that doesn't free us either. That kind of approach might offer immediate satisfaction, but it doesn't offer long-term sustenance of health and freedom.

Below are two helpful resources to find grounding when your body feels overwhelmed, either while you're trying to notice, pause, and allow or just in general.

The 5-4-3-2-1 Exercise: Look around you and name five things you can see, four things you can feel (on your skin), three things you can hear, two things you can smell, and one thing you can taste. Observing your environment in this way can help slow your body down and bring you back into the present moment gently.

The Resource Spot: No matter how distressed your body feels, there is always one part of it that is neutral or calm. It could be a toe, an arm, or your butt in the chair, but no matter how small, some part of your body holds neutrality or calm that can help ground you. Scan your body quickly from head to toe, looking for a part of you that feels neutral, comfortable, or calm. When you find it, shift your attention there and imagine that with each inhale your breath goes directly to that place. And with each exhale, you pull that neutrality or calm throughout the rest of your body. Repeat this until your body feels more grounded.

WHAT THE ENNEAGRAM IS NOT

There are many misconceptions with the Enneagram, its purpose, and how to work with it. Think of the following list as a Frequently Asked Questions section where we look briefly at what the Enneagram is not.

A SYSTEM OF BOXES TO PLACE PEOPLE IN

On the contrary, the Enneagram shows us how our belief that we are our types or ego structures has limited our sense of self, and it offers us a way *out* of the boxes we've been existing in.

A DESCRIPTION OF WHO WE ARE

The Enneagram shows us patterns we have used to survive and seek satisfaction. We utilize our survival patterns, but our survival patterns are not who we are.

A LIST OF BEHAVIORAL TRAITS THAT IDENTIFY A "TYPE" OF PERSON

The Enneagram focuses on the core motivation beneath behavior, not simply on behavior. Core motivation is harder to immediately identify externally, which is why working with the Enneagram requires internal self-observation. It is also why we don't label people or tell them what type we think they are based on a few things we see them do.

THE ENNEAGRAM FOR BLACK LIBERATION

In addition, focusing on behavior and dismissing the context from which it is formed is a tactic of systems of supremacy. An obsession with behavior can sometimes serve as a distraction from the real inequities or injustices that give rise to the behavior. For example, labeling a Black woman as "angry" or "aggressive" and insisting she soften her tone before she can be listened to distracts from the context that birthed her anger.

A MARKER OF WHO IS HEALTHY AND WHO ISN'T

Let's get this out of the way here: the language of healthy versus unhealthy types is wildly unhelpful and introduces a hierarchy that serves our supremacist, capitalist systems but does not serve our liberation. This hierarchy introduces shame into our exploration of type structure, and shame never motivates positive movement toward growth. Shame simply keeps us stuck in feeling bad about how we've shown up in the world.

Rather than labeling people's behavior in this binary of healthy versus unhealthy, I encourage a shift toward conscious versus unconscious, or awake versus asleep. Waking up to ourselves and becoming more human is an ongoing process that requires intentionality and practice.

A STATIC SYSTEM; IT ACCOUNTS FOR THE COMPLEXITIES OF BEING HUMAN

The Enneagram is a dynamic system that accounts for changes under different circumstances—when we are stressed and when we feel secure, our experiences in our family culture, what our experiences of trauma taught us, and so much more. This is why two people who identify as the same type can behave in such wildly different ways from each other. The map of the Enneagram still offers helpful direction, no matter how different and varied our life experiences are.

HOW TO READ THE MAP

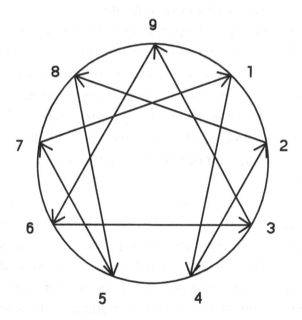

The word *Enneagram* is derived from the Greek *ennea,* meaning nine, and *gram,* meaning text, drawing, or line. As you can see above, the map has nine points around a circle, connected via lines. Each of those nine points corresponds to one of the ego or type structures on the Enneagram and its distinct core motivation. Each type has a basic belief about what is required for survival and satisfaction, which determines what that type pays attention to and avoids. Each type has a certain relationship with other points around the circle. Wings are the numbers that sit right next to your type. I like to think of them as neighbors—you can easily go over and borrow some salt when you run out at home. In the same way, a person with the Type Nine structure can borrow characteristics from both Eight and One that help support their core motivation.

Lines connect each type to two different points on the circle. This is a much more dynamic movement than just going next door to borrow salt. These lines show how we tend to move when we are under stress versus when we feel secure. The line moving away from your type identifies the direction you go when in stress, while the line moving toward your type identifies the direction you go when you feel secure.

These movements via line are often unconscious. Recognizing that you have moved in the direction of stress, for example, is a helpful invitation to pause and notice without judgment while offering compassion to your experience. It is not cause for alarm to recognize you are acting differently under stress. Instead, it is helpful information that can allow you to offer the soothing your body actually needs.

At the same time, these movements can occur consciously if we so choose. We can consciously move in either direction on the lines to borrow from those types' helpful traits for our own growth. For example, a Two believes they must be needed to be loved, which requires them to deny their own needs and focus on what other people want from them. Under stress, Twos might unconsciously move toward point Eight, exploding in anger at others after the Two experiences the consequences of their own poor boundaries. However, a conscious move from Two to Eight offers the Two the ability to be more direct about their needs, take up space, and be honest in their relationships.

The fluidity of the system reminds us of our access to resources outside of our own singular stories. Even though these movements do not change our primary type structures, they can offer us access points to other ways of being that allow us to live more expansively.

POWER AND VULNERABILITY

WHAT IS POWER?

Growing up in my collectivist Nigerian culture, I was raised by a single mother, and I was the only one in my small circle of friends who did not have both parents at home. For a woman to be unmarried with children was a thing of shame because the cultural belief was that being chosen by a man was what legitimized your value as a woman. Even though my parents' divorce was in large part due to my father's behavior, my mother was the one who faced the societal repercussions of being husbandless.

I wasn't consciously aware of the stigma, though, because I thought of my mom as a superhero. She was many things—a writer, a philanthropist, an entrepreneur, a pastor, a keynote speaker who was invited to come speak in many countries on the continent of Africa and abroad. At one point, she started a program to empower and financially support the forgotten widows in her family's village. She supplied them with yards of fabric and a handful of sewing machines and paid for them to learn how to sew so they could earn their own income and move toward financial stability. She still provides them with fabric each year and food staples each quarter. When she heard of a remote village near the border of Nigeria and the Republic of Benin where there wasn't yet a school for the children, she started a school and convinced teachers to go to that remote village and teach the kids how to read and write. She was—and still is—always seeking ways to make it easier for people to access opportunities that she had to fight to get for herself.

When I think of what it means to embody power, I think of my mother. Although she lives in a society—and comes from a family—in which power is often used to dominate and control, she has chosen to use her personal agency to make room for others. Even though she's had to fight to be taken just as seriously as men are in her field of work, she chooses to wield her power in the service of community care and collaboration.

When we generally think of power, we might think of the ability to influence others or the course of events. Power, in social justice work, is also thought of as "the ability to decide who [has] access to resources." This common understanding of power is better thought of as **power over**. This type of power requires control and dominance; it requires taking power away from some in order for others to have it. In this way, power is seen as scarce—a finite resource of which there isn't enough for everyone.

Most of us living in the United States (and in many other societies around the world), tend to believe that power is a finite resource. The systems of power tend to favor those who are centered—white, cisgender, heterosexual, able-bodied, neurotypical, Protestant Christian. In many ways, these identities are considered the norm, or the baseline from which other identities deviate—and often are punished for deviating. Those at the center do not have to fight for access to resources in the same way those furthest away from the center have to. The more power a person holds, the more choices and access to resources are available to them.

Of course, no one holds just a singular identity, and the intersection of different identities can shift where a person lives in relation to the center and how much access to resources they have. A person who lives further away from the center—for example, a Black trans woman—has less power to access resources or decide who has access to resources. Those closer to the margins of the circle have to fight for the resources to simply live, resources that are almost guaranteed for those in the center by the systems that are set up to protect them.

In systems built on power over, those who hold the most power tend to show the strongest resistance to sharing their power. This is because the story of power over involves winners and losers. If one person gives up any bit of their power over, they have "lost" and someone else has won. And since power is seen as a finite resource, losing means you might never get access to power again.

But there are other ways to look at power: **power within** and **power with**. Power within refers to our individual sense of self-worth and agency. Like my mother's deep belief in her own worth and capacity to effect change, power within is the capacity to imagine with hope that my individual actions hold the potential to shift things.

Power with, on the other hand, refers to our collective power. It is based on mutual support, solidarity, and collaboration. The connection between our personal sense of power and agency combined with our collaborative power makes it possible for us to create a new world, one in which we do not recreate the power structures of the oppressors when we are centered. This power is regenerative, communal, sustainable. It is tempting to think of power as only real when it is hierarchical. We have been taught to believe that. But not only can we create systems of healing and justice using power with, we can also create more space for one another to heal and rest.

During the COVID-19 pandemic that spread across the world in 2020, we saw the rise of mutual aid networks. These were communities of people who recognized that the systems we exist in would not step in to offer help and resources to those who needed it. So they took matters into their own hands, organizing collaborative efforts to address the inequities that exist without waiting for a savior. People delivered groceries and medicine to the most vulnerable who were trapped at home. People showed up and acted as medics during protests where those raising their voices against injustice were brutalized by the police. People raised money for those who had lost their jobs and spent their time making and distributing masks. These are examples of power with in action—these beautiful movements that support our collective wellness through collaboration and solidarity.

Unfortunately, in a society structured on power over, the language of healing, wellness, and self-development work can cater only to those in the center and can be damaging for the rest of us who do not have the power to access the resources we need. As we explored in chapter 1, those whose identities offer them more power tend to be the ones who get to define, culturally, what health or wellness is. Those definitions are often feel-good mantras that require no real work to dismantle the systems of white supremacy, patriarchy, and capitalism that harm us every day.

How, then, do those who hold marginalized identities practice healing and rest within systems of oppression? By exercising our power within and power with, it becomes possible to rest and heal while still working to create a more just world in which everybody has access to the resources they need to thrive.

I watched a short video in which Andre Henry, a writer and activist, used the game of Simon Says to illustrate the magnitude of collective power. If you aren't familiar with the way Simon Says works, one person is designated as Simon, and this person tells the group what to do using the formula: "Simon says _____." Group members are only required to do what Simon says, so you have to pay attention to whether the instruction is prefaced by "Simon says" or you lose.

In this video with Andre Henry, the first few rounds of Simon Says were easy—Simon said to do things like "put your hand on your ear" or "clap three times." But then Simon told the audience to punch their neighbors as hard as they could in the stomach. Everyone laughed and no punching happened. He repeated the command, and still no one obeyed. Though he was the authority in that room, the one on stage with a microphone, the people's collective power outweighed his harmful instructions. What Andre Henry was illustrating was this: it is our obedience to the dictates of oppressive systems that maintains the status quo. The systems need our cooperation and compliance in order to thrive.

With our collective power, we can opt out of the metaphorical game of Simon Says in order to protect our own and one another's well-being. We don't have to wait for permission from the powers that be to see our lives, our rest, and our joy as worthy of protecting. This changes the way we show up and organize to dismantle and disrupt systems of oppression.

VULNERABILITY AND POWER

You might be wondering why I have a chapter on power in a book about the Enneagram. Well, in my training to become a certified teacher and practitioner of the Enneagram, my internal alarm bells would go off every time my teachers would define the movement toward growth as essentially a movement toward greater vulnerability.

We all come into the world with unconscious, hidden vulnerabilities. When we experience pain in our formative years, we become aware of some of those vulnerabilities.

Our brains and bodies begin to create patterns to protect us from reexperiencing pain, and these ongoing patterns of behavior become our type structures, which operate unconsciously in the background to keep us safe from external threats. What I was taught was that growth involves seeing the patterns we built up to protect our vulnerabilities as a necessary part of childhood development—but less necessary now. My interpretation of these definitions was that the healthy life is one lived without armor.

That definition works really well, and is actually important work, for centered people. However, there is a difference between an imagined threat and an actual threat to safety. For those whose perception of unsafety is constructed by systems of oppression, learning to separate the false story from what is real is necessary work. If a white woman grew up with the story that Black men are dangerous and scary, she might unconsciously organize her life around what she believes will keep her safe. She might choose to live in a predominantly white neighborhood, avoid the "dangerous" parts of town, clutch her purse and cross the street if she sees a Black man approaching.

The armor she's created to keep herself safe is based on a false story. We know her safety isn't actually in jeopardy because Black men exist. But her armor is absolutely real, and the power with which she wields that armor makes it less safe for other folks to thrive. This is why we are inundated with news stories about white women or police officers who believe their lives are in danger in proximity to Black people and end up causing harm, often death. For centered people, it is necessary work to unlearn the patterns built up in their formative years and interrogate the stories they tell themselves about what it means to be safe, loved, and worthy of belonging. Setting down their armor and embracing vulnerability *is* necessary work.

But that is not my work. The threats to my safety and my well-being are very real, and I have limited access to the kind of protection and privilege that is afforded those in the center. It is extremely privileged to define the healthy life as one without armor. Defining it in such a way caters best to those who do not face direct harm by laying down their armor. It is harmful to make unarmored vulnerability the end goal without addressing the systemic inequities that make armoring necessary for groups of people.

Power and vulnerability work hand in hand. With an increase in power, there tends to be an increase in a person's capacity to conceal their vulnerabilities. There are two ways to think about vulnerability that are helpful for our purposes. The first is to define it as our capacity to be affected by external sources, which is a natural condition of humanity—something we all share. The second is to consider that some have "reduced capacity, power, or control to protect their interests relative to other agents." In other words, some of us are more vulnerable than others, depending on our proximity to the center.

Many people who hold marginalized identities often exist with their vulnerabilities on full display without choice or control. If aspects of your identity that you have no control over—skin color, sexual orientation, gender—are threatened in some way by the external world, your vulnerabilities in those areas are always revealed, even if you want them hidden sometimes. The ability to willfully conceal vulnerability requires power, and power is concentrated in the center. Those who are centered are protected by the system and, therefore, face less harm by embracing vulnerability.

The growth work for Black, Indigenous, and non-Black People of Color is not the same as the growth work for those who are centered. If we are living with our vulnerabilities constantly exposed and facing harm because of it, our work is *not*, then, to lean further into more exposure and risk. Our work is not simply to set down the armor but to build awareness of self separate from armor, so we can be free to make a choice as to when to hold up the armor and when to lower it in safe spaces. In this way we can still live with freedom while we do the work to liberate ourselves from the systems of oppression. If we don't learn how to do that, we can confuse our identities with the armor so much so that we become unable to access safety within ourselves. But it is exhausting work, and we cannot ask people who face the greatest risk in a society to set down their armor without first asking those with the weapons to give them up.

For those who are centered, your work is to look at the ways in which your armor can make it difficult for others within the circle to set down theirs because you have access to more power and control by being in the center. In the service of collective growth and liberation, it is necessary to talk about why armor is needed for those who live further away from the center and to ask—especially if you hold identities that are centered—"In what ways do I participate in the harm that requires that person to keep their armor up?" If it is true that no one is free until we all are free, then the illusion of freedom that being in the center gives you is just that—a delusion. Real freedom includes all of us.

THE WORK OF HEALING

It is a less complicated process to heal a wound that was inflicted one time and can be cleaned and covered to protect it from further harm. A wound that remains open with no protection *and* also repeatedly gets bumped, poked, scratched, and so on never fully heals. When the systems that Black folks live in repeatedly harm them, setting down the armor as a way of leaning into vulnerability is not the path to freedom and healing. In many ways, the armor increases our resilience and our capacity to survive these inequitable systems. But remember that the goal of liberation is not merely survival; it is our full thriving. Carrying around heavy armor all the time, and confusing our true identities with the armor we carry, doesn't support our freedom.

So what does healing and wholeness look like in the middle of a fight in which your armor is necessary because you are a target? How do you heal from the trauma of knowing you are always a target no matter how educated, unthreatening, and amiable you present yourself to be? The work of healing and wholeness for Black folks and others on the margins in our society must include practices that do not require us to expose ourselves to more harm in the name of wellness and growth. Growth is neither consenting to systems of harm nor pretending that they do not exist. For those of us who face more harm by taking off our armor, our work is to learn how to exercise choice to wield the armor as a tool rather than confuse it with our identity. In doing so, we find freedom while the battle rages on.

Paying attention to our bodies, and creating a sense of safety within ourselves especially in a world that doesn't offer us safety, gives us more access to the space between who we are and the armor we carry. That allows us to choose when to put down the armor and allow our soft selves to be seen. In spaces that do not offer safety, we can choose to—without shame—pick up the parts of our armor that keep us protected. In safe spaces, where love is being offered, we can take off our armor and receive tending and care. And when we make space for ourselves to heal, we metabolize our pain rather than transmit it to those around us or those that come after us.

PART
2

Chapter 4

A GUIDE TO EXPLORING THE ENNEAGRAM

As we move through the next nine chapters that focus on individual types, we will be using two important frameworks within the Enneagram, the centers of intelligence and the defense system.

THE CENTERS OF INTELLIGENCE

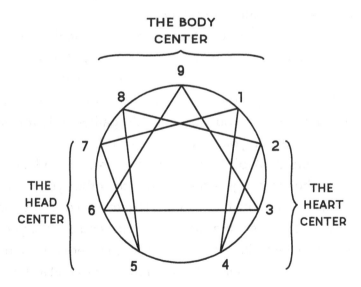

THE BODY CENTER

THE HEAD CENTER

THE HEART CENTER

The circle of the Enneagram is divided into three centers of intelligence, which we all possess. These three centers—Body, Heart, and Head—hold wisdom that, when integrated, can help us live more consciously embodied lives. Our exploration of type structures in the following chapters will be organized around centers, and we'll explore the centers' core needs and core emotions before diving into type-specific information.

As a brief introduction to the centers of intelligence, it is helpful to know that each type is located within one center. The Body Center comprises types Eight, Nine, and One, and these types are most concerned with issues of worth and belonging. The Heart Center contains types Two, Three, and Four, and these types are most concerned with issues of love and approval. And the Head Center contains types Five, Six, and Seven, and these types are most concerned with issues of security and safety.

Whichever center your type is located in is the center that is most comfortable and familiar to you. It is the one you overuse while underusing the others. One of my teachers refers to it as your area of familiar suffering. Your dominant center is where you most naturally gather and process information to help you navigate the world.

You could think of the centers as a three-legged stool. If one of the three legs is shorter than the other, you would most likely lean on the shorter leg to avoid wobbling around. In doing so, the other two legs would lift slightly and lose contact with the ground. The goal here is to bring these centers into balance, to live in such a way that all three legs of the stool are connected to the ground of reality. We want to harness the wisdom of the head, heart and body to help us live a more integrated life.

As we explore the types, we will begin each section with the type in the middle of that intelligence triad: Nine, Three, and Six. This is because these types, also known as the central triangle, are thought to have the clearest depiction of the main themes of that center. If you are unsure which type is home base for you, you can start by reading the introduction to each center and exploring the three types within the center that resonates most with you.

THE DEFENSE SYSTEM

If our Enneagram types are armor, the defense system is the material that makes up that armor. Because wielding our armor is usually subconscious, we are often unaware of the defense system or the subtle ways in which it works to keep the stories of our types in place. The defense system contains three parts, all essential for the continued functioning of our type structures.

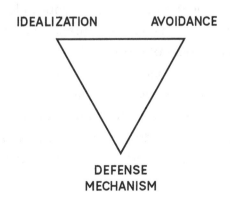

IDEALIZATION   AVOIDANCE

DEFENSE
MECHANISM

The first part of the defense system is the idealization, which is who we believe we *must* be in order to belong, to be loved, and to be safe. The idealization is usually based on attributes that are naturally true about us, and this is what makes up our armor. However, the type structure seizes those attributes and makes a tight fist around them, creating an either-or narrative that says *we have to be this and nothing else, otherwise we'll lose out on belonging, love, and safety.* We create an idealized version of ourselves that we believe is what makes us worthy of that belonging, love, and safety. If you are naturally optimistic, for example, the type structure might seize that quality and convince you that you *must* be optimistic at all times in order to remain safe in a world filled with pain. You might judge yourself if you do not meet this expectation of being optimistic in every situation.

The second part of the defense system is the avoidance, which is often the opposite of the idealization. If the story we're working with says that you can only be one thing in order to be okay, anything contrary to that one thing is seen by your type structure as a threat to your belonging, love, and safety. In order to avoid these threats, the type structure pushes the awareness of these attributes into the shadows of our subconscious, making it easier to believe that those things aren't true about us. It's similar to focusing a camera lens on the subject we want to capture, effectively blurring out everything else we don't want to see. And yet, ignoring or avoiding certain parts of ourselves does not make them go away. Even from the background, the parts of ourselves we avoid still exert a huge influence on our behavior and our relationships with self and others. To continue with the previous example, if you *must* be optimistic to be safe, experiences with pain and suffering will be avoided at all costs, and the parts of you that do feel pain will be relegated to the shadows in order to maintain your optimism about life.

The final part of the defense system is the defense mechanism, which works hard to keep the split between the idealization and the avoidance. Like a computer always running in the background, it constantly monitors when you are leaning too far in the direction of the avoidance and snaps you back to the idealized story. The defense mechanism is the enforcer of the idealized story. For example, since no one can effectively avoid all pain and suffering, the defense mechanism of rationalizing makes it such that you can explain away the pain in order to focus on positive possibilities instead.

The work of integration involves moving toward the things that scare us and befriending our shadow selves. While the subjective reality of our types convinces us that life is either idealization or avoidance, the objective reality is that the fullness of our humanity includes both our idealizations *and* our avoidances without threatening our worthiness, lovability, and security. In moving toward what scares us, we can begin to pry open that tight fist around the subjective story. We start to experience more acceptance and an increased capacity to soothe our fears while embracing the parts of ourselves we used to believe made us less worthy. When we can bring awareness to our defense mechanisms and how they operate, we have more power to slow down the rapid firing of our patterns so we can exercise choice about what stories we believe about who we are.

Chapter 5
THE BODY CENTER

**THE BODY
CENTER**

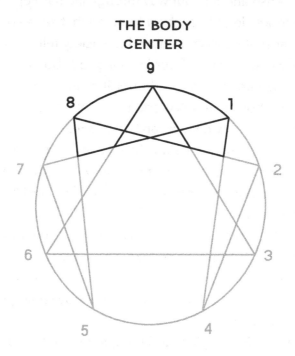

The Body Center of intelligence is the seat of our felt-sense knowing. Through the body, we gather information about the world through physical sensations, gut responses, and instincts. Our bodies take in eleven million bits of information *per second*, while our conscious minds are only able to process fifty bits per second. This is another reason why we need an integrated wisdom because we miss so much of our experience when we only elevate the wisdom of the head.

In our Western world, Black women and Indigenous folks in particular are socialized to disregard our bodies' wisdom in favor of the linear, cognitive theories of knowing. Being able to sense and feel our way through life has kept us safe, but often we don't know how to name that sense of knowing because it doesn't fit into what society tells us wisdom is. Or if we are aware of our knowing—our bodies' intuitive wisdom—we are hesitant to honor it or let it guide us. But our bodies hold so much wisdom and information that help us make sense of what we can't often see.

The Body Center sorts this felt-sense information in very binary ways—good or bad, right or wrong, pain or pleasure. There is an either-or approach to life found here, and exploring the gray area is difficult for Body types. Often quick judgments are made—"I like it" or "I don't like it." It can be difficult to pause or take a step back to be curious about the middle ground because the quick judgment has already been made, led by the strong body feeling that has already occurred.

For types Eight, Nine, and One, found in the Body Center, the focus of attention is on personal power and control. Body types use their position and power to make life the way they believe it *should* be. Being in control of one's self and one's environment is very important to this triad.

Body types are also very values driven, and living with integrity connected to those values is very important to them. While they may not let it show very much on the outside, they are usually very connected to their own vulnerabilities. This is why they focus on using their personal power to keep themselves protected. They tend to fear being blindsided or swept away either by others or by their own strong feelings, so they spend a lot of their time ensuring they can remain in control. When they find themselves not in control or losing control, Eights feel aggravated, Nines feel overwhelmed, and Ones feel resentful.

The core needs of the types in this center are for **belonging**, power, control, worth, autonomy, respect, and boundaries. Power, control, respect and worth are seen as prerequisites or determinants of belonging, which is at the core of what they seek. Body types use their personal power to ensure that they remain worthy of belonging.

When these needs are threatened, the core emotion that arises is anger. Anger makes sense if we think of someone trying to control us, violate a boundary, or threaten our belonging. Anger is expressed differently through each of the three Body types, though. Anger in Eights is often expressed as rage, in Nines as passive-aggressive stubbornness, and in Ones as resentment.

The anger of Eights and Ones tends to move them into action. In the Body Center's binary view of the world, you are either a winner or a loser, victorious or vanquished. So this anger propels Eights and Ones into the battle they see as inevitable, with a determination to not give away any of their power or control.

For Nines, the battle is more internal as they believe that expressing their anger might lead to them losing control over themselves and in turn giving away control to the other. In response to that fear they tamp down on their anger, sometimes convincing themselves that it is not even there as a way to maintain control over the self.

Overall, this triad is concerned with who they are and who holds the power in their lives. Eights tend to move more assertively outward to expand their boundaries of power, while Ones tend to contract in order to comply with the "correct" standards of behavior. Nines tend to blur the boundaries between themselves and others, merging with the expectations of others as a way to hold on to their sense of belonging.

When people in this triad are able to come home to who they truly are and remember their inherent worth, they are able to participate in reality as it is without constantly trying to resist or defend against it.

Chapter 6
TYPE NINE: ADAPTABILITY AS ARMOR

NICKNAMES	The Mediator, The Peacemaker
ARMOR	Adaptability
HOLY IDEA	Love
VIRTUE/ESSENCE QUALITY	Right Action
MENTAL HABIT	Self-forgetting
EMOTIONAL HABIT	Laziness Towards Self

HOLY IDEA

HOLY LOVE: The Table of Belonging

Imagine your best friend invites you over for a dinner party. Everyone you love is invited too—family and friends, all enjoying one another's company and hopefully still getting along even after a few glasses of wine. Imagine that when you show up to this dinner party, there is a long table set with intention and thoughtfulness. A place card with the name of the person whose seat it is rests on each plate. Everything is laid out beautifully and invitingly. You're one of the first to arrive, and you find a place card with your name on it and begin to settle in. No matter how the rest of the evening unfolds, your spot at the table is always secure. You are wanted in this room, and you can take up space because there is enough for everybody.

This is a depiction of **Holy Love**—the objective reality, or Holy Idea, associated with the Type Nine structure. Within the reality of Holy Love, *everything and everyone belongs equally in a state of union that isn't severed by what we do or fail to do.* Holy Love says that we belong at the table as our full selves, with our complicated thoughts and feelings, with our anger and our tenderness, our gifts and our challenges. We belong at the table because we are loved, and we are loved simply because we exist. There is nothing we can do to change our standing; there is no way we can earn our belonging at the table and, therefore, no way we can un-earn it. This knowing frees us up to be fully present, to experience the love that is always and has always been there for us. It gives us the courage to take our rightful seats at the table of belonging and experience the breadth and depth of connection that is only possible when we aren't hiding ourselves in the corner.

When Nines are disconnected from Holy Love, they start to believe that they have to earn their spots at the table by shrinking themselves to be as adaptable and easygoing as possible. Their energy then goes toward pleasing other people, keeping the room comfortable and conflict-free, and forgetting about themselves in the process. A Nine notices that it's a little too warm in the room, so they open a window. Another person asks for ice in their water, and the Nine offers to grab it while throwing out an anecdote that would help Cousin A and Friend B find something interesting to talk about that connects them. And it seems to work—in fact, it works so well that the Nine wonders if it wouldn't be better to just hang out in the corner, responding to people's needs and helping diffuse any conflict that arises from a safe distance. This way, they can avoid saying the wrong thing or offending anyone. Because what if they do and are no longer invited to any future dinner parties or hangouts?

In order to avoid losing connection and facing separation, Nines tell themselves that the safest place in the room is the corner. Even if it requires them to shrink themselves into smaller quarters, it allows them to remain in the room and not get kicked out. It gives them proximity to a counterfeit form of connection that lets them avoid the risk required to be fully seen. Nines forget that there is already a place card with their name on it at the table, a place for them that cannot be earned or lost.

Knowing that you belong inherently and are loved unequivocally allows you to open up to risk. And for those with the Type Nine structure, who have come to believe that they must shrink themselves in order to belong, Holy Love offers the invitation to rise from the corner of the room and take their seats at the table. When a Nine is connected to Holy Love, they exude the virtue termed **right action**, which is the bodily experience of taking action that honors yourself as equal to—not more than or less than—others. Right action allows Nines to reconnect with their own sense of agency in order to bring the fullness of who they are to their everyday lives.

IDEALIZATION

Peaceful, Agreeable, Adaptable

Our armor is formed as a result of real experiences of pain and suffering. When people experience disconnection or separation as a result of taking up space or being fully themselves early in life, they learn that their sense of belonging is only secure when they go with the flow and keep things easy and conflict-free. If the Nine type structure is your home base, you subconsciously create an armor that is agreeable and adaptable to help you blend in and maintain the connection and belonging you desire. You frequently demote your needs and desires to keep the peace.

Often, Nines felt during childhood like there wasn't enough room for them to take up space because there was already a lot of conflict and chaos or because others' personalities in their family systems were more overpowering. Nines feel a strong sense of being overlooked, which then teaches them to go along with the plans already set in motion by others so as to keep a positive connection and not be forgotten completely.

Nines often come across as peaceful, nonconfrontational, adaptable, and thoughtful. They want to ensure that they are liked by others so that they don't get kicked out of belonging, and they do this by being sensitive to others while shrinking themselves to keep the peace. They are incredibly sensitive to their environments because so much of their energy is subconsciously spent managing the external environment to gain a sense of control and comfort. Remember the dinner party? A Nine in that space is picking up on everyone's feelings and needs constantly, so much so that it makes it hard to know what is true of their individual experience and what is simply true of the environment. They may wonder, *"Am I uncomfortable with the conversation going on around me, or am I picking up on someone else's discomfort and confusing it as my own? Do I really enjoy this activity, or am I going along with it because I know the person I'm with really enjoys it?"*

In short, a Nine's attention is habitually focused on others and their environment more than their internal experience, and this pattern creates a mental habit of **self-forgetting**. It is this habit of forgetting themselves that keeps Nines so adaptable. They merge so fully with others that it becomes easy to forget that they have an identity separate from the other person or the group. This is their way to find belonging in a world they believe doesn't offer equal space for everyone to belong.

Comfort is an incredibly important part of the armor for Nines. They seek to maintain comfort by creating harmony in their relationships and environments. They tell themselves that the best way to achieve that harmonious, peaceful life is to go with the flow and avoid rocking the boat. Nines also seek comfort through routines and structure. The preference for routines can be helpful except when it acts as a mechanism to lull you to sleep. For example, when you've driven the same route between work and home every day for months, eventually you can do it without being present at all. You get in the car at work and walk into your home however many minutes later without any memory of navigating your way home. This experience is an example of how people within the Nine type structure develop a habit of falling asleep to who they are and what is most important to them. With routines, it is easy to fall asleep to life and operate on autopilot. This keeps life comfortable, predictable, and, ideally, free of conflict.

Being adaptable means being able to adjust easily, whether it's to a change of plans or a new direction or something someone asks of me. It means not asking for too much or being too demanding, or it means taking up as little space as possible to not be an inconvenience. I usually can make any situation work, and there is a positive side to being adaptable that has made me a really good employee in my workplace. This flexibility has also helped me make lots of different kinds of friends. The not-so-positive side is that I can accommodate everyone else's needs so much that I end up in uncomfortable situations I don't want to be in because I just went along with other people's plans. I try to be palatable and easygoing, even when I might be annoyed or irritated at someone.

—Ashley

AVOIDANCE

Conflict, Discomfort, Anger

If you believe that you have to be adaptable, easygoing, and peaceful in order to be worthy of belonging, then your type structure will try to avoid conflict, discomfort, and anger at all costs. Underneath a Nine's avoidance is a core fear of **separation**. The Nine story says: your worth and belonging is directly tied to how unobtrusive and adaptable you are. Therefore, if people experience you as taking up too much space—creating conflict, making things uncomfortable, showing anger—your right to belong will be revoked.

This is the exact messaging our society gives to Black folks all the time. The armor of a Nine is necessary in this sense because external belonging is predicated on it. Being easygoing, adaptable, and not asking for too much in certain unsafe spaces can often be the difference between life and death for Black folks. Disconnecting ourselves from what we really need or even from our anger can be a necessary strategy to avoid harm. But if we confuse our identities with the armor, we lose contact with our truest selves and begin to shape our sense of self around what others require of us.

The word *conflict* can conjure up images of dramatic arguments or stony silences, but something as simple as being invited to share their own perspective on a topic can register as conflict in a Nine's body. Often, Nines tell me that it takes a lot of energy to share an opinion because they believe they have to be prepared to defend that position if others don't automatically agree with it. Nines often fear that they don't have the ability to defend their stance and that trying to do so will lead to conflict and potential relational separation. So rather than share an opinion, they go along to get along.

Even though Nines project an appearance of being easygoing, they experience anger like all of us. Almost every time I ask Nines about their relationship to anger, they assert that they aren't angry people and never really get angry. This is because the Nine experience of anger is often referred to as "anger that's been put to sleep." This anger comes across through passive-aggressive tendencies. If you ask a Nine to do something for you that they have no willingness nor intention to do, they might smile and agree to your request, knowing full well that they will not do it. Every time you ask them about it, they will seem very apologetic about how they forgot to do it because so many other things have been going on. This pattern will continue until eventually you fight about it and/or do it yourself. Saying no to the request the first time feels like uncomfortable conflict to a Nine, and so they say yes to something they can't or won't do, which inevitably leads to the very conflict they were trying to avoid in the first place.

Sometimes, the Nine isn't aware in the moment that they don't want to or don't have the capacity to fulfill the other person's request. They only realize it in retrospect, when the actual work of showing up is required. They might feel resentful toward the other person, feeling as though they are being forced into something they don't want to do, even though they have the agency to say no.

Often, Nines distance themselves from their anger because they don't believe their anger is as valid as others'. They tend to only bring up their anger or frustration when they've reached a ten, and at that point, they might list off all of the things you've been doing that have bothered them for months. In reality, Nines' experience of anger or frustration is valid, even at a one on the scale, but due to their own fear that others will invalidate their anger, they preemptively invalidate it themselves. Paying attention to their anger is the most direct route to reconnecting with themselves. Seeing anger as an invitation to pay attention to the need underneath the anger can teach Nines to forget themselves less and honor their needs more.

Nines also get distracted by the inessentials as a way to avoid conflict and keep the peace. For a Nine, the most important thing is whatever is in front of them in that moment, even if there are more important tasks to get done. If a challenging conversation needs to be had with a friend or significant other, for example, it is quite likely that the Nine might become consumed with a need to clean the entire house or work on the yard immediately. This pattern diverts their attention from the most important thing until the moment passes. This way, they avoid the uncomfortable conversation.

I want everything in my life to be as comfortable as possible. If I'm traveling, I'll pack clothes for every possible situation so that I can be comfortable no matter the temperature in the house or the weather outside. I honestly love being in my own home because it's so comfortably the way I like it. That's one way I avoid conflict, by making sure I prioritize being comfortable. If I'm comfortable, it's easier for me to be chill and open minded. When someone is upset with me, it's really stressful because I immediately want to fix it and get back to being okay. I can get really defensive because I don't want to be the person who's responsible for creating the conflict, so sometimes that stubbornness and defensiveness can make the argument worse. Sometimes I'm passive-aggressive instead of saying what I really mean because I don't want my true feelings (like anger) to hurt the other person even more.

When I think of disconnection because of something I did or said, I feel hot and sweaty. My throat tightens up, and my stomach is in knots. I feel like my body is compressing, as if I'm steeling myself for a fight.

—Ashley

DEFENSE MECHANISM

Numbing

The defense mechanism that keeps this type structure going is called narcotization, or simply, numbing. This refers to the pattern of using routines, food, comfort, and other people's agendas as a form of anesthesia to keep you unaware of what is important and real. Numbing is like taking a literal chill pill that allows Nines to show up in their lives as a subdued version of themselves that they believe will be easier for others to get along with.

There are two ways numbing shows up. High-energy Nines numb through activity. They stay busy whether at home, in the groups they are part of, or with their significant relationships. These Nines are often on the go and use their busy schedules and routines as an easy way to run on autopilot. If you have six meetings back-to-back today and get home with only enough time to eat dinner before it's bedtime, then there is no time left to pay attention to what's really going on inside of you or what you need. For these Nines, routine is sacred because it keeps them insulated from the discomfort of being fully present.

Low-energy Nines, on the other hand, numb through the usual suspects that may come to mind—food, alcohol, television, and comfort. For example, it is much more comfortable to watch a few episodes of a show with a glass of wine each night than to look your partner in the eye and have a conversation about your relationship or each other. For these Nines, maintaining a comfortable equilibrium takes precedence over telling the truth to themselves.

Nines can utilize both high-energy and low-energy tactics when they need to, but usually they find that one of these two is their most comfortable go-to. What is true across the board is that when a Nine begins to lean too far into conflict, discomfort, or anger, the defense mechanism of numbing kicks in to pull them back into being adaptable, easygoing, and peaceful.

As a result of the story that says you have to go with the flow to find belonging, Nines develop an emotional habit of **laziness** toward their own priorities and needs. This laziness refers to a lack of contact with the self; it is not about a lack of productivity or energy for life as a whole. Nines have a certain laziness toward figuring out who they really are and what they really need, let alone advocating for those needs or asserting themselves in the world. Many Nines feel as though life happens *to* them rather than believing they have agency to make life happen. Over time, this laziness leads to a complete disconnect with themselves so that even when space is made for their needs by others, they might have no idea what those needs are. Often when a Nine is asked what they want, they say they don't know. This habitual (and unconscious) avoidance of what they want helps them preserve a form of comfort and connectedness in relationships.

If I didn't have to be adaptable all the time, I would be more honest and direct. I'd let myself show my anger more, but in an upfront way instead of restricting it. I think I'd be less worried about being my full self if I wasn't worried about the conflict that could cause. I feel like I can only be two ways—either super opinionated and controlling or super chill and easygoing. Only my husband sees the side of me that can be very opinion-ated because I know he isn't going anywhere and I can allow myself to say, *"No, I don't like that"* or *"I don't want to do that."* But with everyone else, I don't want them to see me that way. So if I didn't have to be adaptable all the time, maybe I'd be able to live more in the middle where I can share how I'm really feeling without swing-ing to either controlling or passive.

My armor of adaptability is necessary in a lot of spaces, I think. It's helpful at work because I'm able to take on more responsibility and be flexible with the tasks I'm required to do. It's helpful when I'm around people with whom I might not necessarily see eye to eye; I can usu-ally get along with almost anyone. It's really helpful as a Black woman to be able to be friendly and smile and be perceived as not harmful by people who are wait-ing for any excuse to label me an angry Black woman and dismiss me. It's hard to know when my armor isn't necessary because I feel like it's such a positive thing to be able to be so adaptable most of the time. But I think in situations that would benefit from me being more direct, or from me saying no and having better bound-aries, adaptability isn't helpful. With people, like my hus-band, who I feel so safe and understood by, I don't need to be as adaptable and can be more honest about what I need.

—Ashley

CREATING SPACE BETWEEN SELF AND ARMOR

Notice—Pause—Allow

Remember that your practice is to notice, pause, and allow what comes up to be there without judgment or shame. Let compassion, gratitude, and curiosity guide you as you use the following prompts and exercises to practice bringing awareness to your experience of the type structure. Below are some helpful ways to begin noticing the patterns of your type. The stress and security movements and somatic profile can help you begin to practice curiosity when you notice yourself showing up in these ways.

Stress and Security Movements

When Nines are experiencing stress, they move toward Six. A conscious movement to Six can help Nines, who are gifted at seeing all points of view on any given topic, utilize a more selective focus for stressors or conflict they cannot avoid. They might zero in their focus on the problems or worst-case scenarios of their current stressors, make pro and con lists, and identify their alternatives. This can help a Nine to make a decision about the next steps to take or the right course of action. The unconscious movement to Six can present a challenge for Nines in that they might get stuck in anxiety, information gathering, and consensus-seeking behavior. They might also delay action because they think they don't have all the necessary information to proceed.

When Nines are relaxed and feel secure, they move toward the more energetic space of the Three. A conscious movement to Three allows a Nine to show up with more presence and active energy, and they are able to respond more quickly to relational and environmental requests. The challenge with an unconscious movement toward Three is that Nines can feel overwhelmed by the heart space's fixation with finding an identity. In the Three space, a Nine can begin to wonder who they really are and what their identity is, which can sometimes feel overwhelming for this type.

Somatic Profile

Nines tend to experience in their bodies what is happening in the environment. A friend of mine who identifies with this type describes it as existing without the top layer of skin. Nines have very permeable boundaries and can become overwhelmed quickly by all the information their bodies are constantly picking up. Since the gut or belly center is where most of their energy resides, it is also where they feel the bodily experience of discomfort or conflict. The lower back in Nines tends to be the area that holds a lot of that tension and discomfort. Knowing this can help Nines use the experience of discomfort in their lower backs as a cue to notice what needs attention, where they might be suppressing anger, what boundaries they need to set or reinforce, and where they are shrinking themselves.

Journal Prompts

Below are some prompts to help you begin to practice curiosity around the story of your type. Find a quiet place to reflect on these questions. Remember to be present with your body as you answer these prompts. Notice, pause, and allow. Be compassionate, curious, and grateful to your body for its intelligence. You can come back to this practice as often as you need to.

1. What is your earliest memory of feeling joyful and free? Where were you? Who were you with? What were you doing? Pause to check in: How does your body feel right now as you write about it?
2. What would change about the way you live if it were true that you don't have to earn your place at the table? Pause to check in: How does your body feel right now as you write about it?
3. What if it's true that you can express your anger, and even experience other people's anger toward you, without losing worth or belonging?
4. If you didn't *have* to be adaptable all the time, who would you be free to be?
5. When is your armor of adaptability necessary in your everyday life? When is it *not* necessary?
6. What does safety feel like in your body? Who do you feel safe with, enough to set down the armor? How does your body feel when you're with that person? Are you feeling some of that safety right now? You can always return to this space within yourself no matter what is happening outside of you.

Visualizations

Find a quiet place where you can relax without worry of interruption. If you are able, sit comfortably upright, uncrossing your hands and placing both feet flat on the floor. If you aren't able to do so, adjust your body to a position that helps you feel comfortable and grounded. Read through the prompt below, then close your eyes and begin to visualize. When you have completed the visualization, slowly bring your attention back to your body and the surface you are resting on, listen to the sounds around you, and open your eyes.

1. Visualize yourself picking up adaptability and putting it on like armor. What does your armor look like? How does your body feel when you are carrying the armor?
2. Visualize yourself taking off the armor of adaptability and setting it down. How does your body feel when you imagine setting down the armor in a safe space?

Community Practice

Often, we subconsciously weaponize our armor against others. If we live by a singular story, we try to subject others to that singular story as well. Because you believe you must be adaptable to have worth and belonging, you might unknowingly require others around you to be adaptable in order to belong. Because you avoid your own anger and internal conflict, you might avoid and/or judge harshly others who readily express their anger or choose discomfort. As you create space between yourself and your armor, I encourage you to consider how you require those around you to fit into your singular story. As you become more comfortable with discomfort and conflict, you will increase your capacity to be with other people's expressions of conflict and anger.

Chapter 7

TYPE EIGHT: STRENGTH AS ARMOR

NICKNAMES	The Protector, The Challenger
ARMOR	Strength
HOLY IDEA	Truth
VIRTUE/ESSENCE QUALITY	Innocence
MENTAL HABIT	Revenge
EMOTIONAL HABIT	Lust

HOLY IDEA

HOLY TRUTH: The Grains of Sand

Imagine you are standing on a beach with your toes in the sand on a warm day. The sand seems endless, stretching out for miles everywhere you look. You scoop up a handful of sand and let the grains fall through your fingers, noticing how identical they all look to the naked eye. As they fall through your fingers, it seems as though there are hundreds of the same little grains spilling back into the millions underneath your feet. At the same time, you know that each of those grains is distinctly different from the rest. If you were to observe each grain of sand under a microscope or magnifying glass, you would see different textures, different colors, and a completely different composition to each one. It is true that when looking with the naked eye, the sand beneath your feet looks homogenous. It is also true that when viewed up close, each grain of sand is distinct in its own particular way. Your perception changes the way you experience reality but doesn't change reality itself.

This is a depiction of **Holy Truth**, the objective reality, or Holy Idea, associated with the Type Eight structure. Holy Truth is *a state of experiencing the multidimensional nature of the undivided oneness that exists in all things in each moment.* It invites us into a nondual experiencing of reality in which we remember that we all can have different perceptions of the same reality without one being more real or true than the other. Like those ambiguous images where one person sees a face while another sees a vase, each perception is real and valid. This means that each of our perceptions carries a measure of truth with it. One of the true things Eights are invited to remember is that, at their core, they are inherently good and worthy of belonging. Nothing they do can change this essential truth about them.

However, when Eights experience pain in their formative years, they lose sight of this inherent goodness and belonging and start to see both themselves and the world as cut off from goodness completely. This becomes their only truth, that the world is harsh and unjust and those with power take advantage of others. It is as though the Eight commits to only one perception of sand, arguing that because sand looks homogenous to the naked eye, it cannot be true that each grain of sand is different from the next. When Eights lose contact with Holy Truth, they begin to see reality through a lens of duality, each believing that their own perception is the only true one. They enforce this perception on others, believing that any other perception that differs from theirs is wrong. They experience this duality internally as well, holding themselves to only one perception of strength and truth while denying what else is real.

When Eights are connected to Holy Truth, they exude the virtue of **innocence**, which is the ability to enter each moment with openness and curiosity, ready to learn from the truth that resides in all beings in each moment. Rather than seeking to enforce their own perspective of truth, innocence allows Eights to enter each moment with a childlike curiosity, ready to discover and marvel at the goodness they find both within themselves and in the world around them.

IDEALIZATION

Strong, Powerful

When Eights become disconnected from Holy Truth, they begin to believe that they must be strong and powerful to protect themselves in a tough and unjust world. This loss of connection to the multidimensional nature of truth creates an either-or duality in Eights that tells them to *eat or be eaten*. As a result, Eights are self-confident, assertive people who like to be in control and get things done. They are direct, authoritative, blunt, and full of big and bold energy. They are passionate people who are prone to "tell it like it is" without mincing words.

Strength as the armor for Eights is multifaceted. Eights have a tough-skinned personality that presents as seemingly impenetrable to pain. They don't tolerate "soft" emotions like sadness or fear, both within themselves and the people around them. To an Eight, possessing strength looks like taking a godlike defiant stance against being affected by the world. They are proud of their ability to remain unaffected and expect the same from others. In addition to a tough personality, literal physical strength also becomes armor for this type. If possible, Eights want strong bodies that can lift and bend and cycle and run as far as they want to because it maintains their story of being powerful. This perception of strength is rigid and inflexible, requiring constant energy to keep oneself tough and hardened at all times. Real strength, on the other hand, is flexible and open. In the words of Confucius, "The green reed which bends in the wind is stronger than the mighty oak which breaks in a storm." This is a potent reminder for Eights whose rigid perception of strength actually presents a greater liability to their well-being.

Being strong to me means you're not emotional and you don't let people know you're hurting. You don't let anyone know anything that they could use against you ever. To be strong means pushing past my body's limits, regardless of how I actually feel or how tired I am. I just keep going. It means not saying no to things that I can do, just because I can do them. If I say no, someone might think that I can't, or I might prove that I can't and that I'm not capable.

—Jessica Denise Dickson

Eights also love to be in control of themselves and their environment. It isn't their intent or desire to be controlling of others; they just don't like feeling controlled. Eights want the freedom to do what works best for them, so they structure their lives in a way that services that desire. The type structure demands that they are always in the driver's seat, regardless of whose car it is. This can create a "my way or the highway" type of personality, which others inevitably experience as controlling.

Having big energy is one of the easily identifiable characteristics of this type. Eights bring their big, zestful energy for life everywhere they go. They bring the full force of their presence to every situation, whether or not it calls for it. Imagine that there is a brick on the ground in front of you that I ask you to pick up. Visualize yourself bending down to pick up that brick—how much energy or strength it takes as you lift it up from the ground and return to standing. Now do it again, except this time, imagine there's a feather on the ground in front of you that I ask you to pick up. Visualize the amount of energy and strength it takes to pick up the feather and return to standing. Picking up a feather requires significantly different energy than picking up a brick. Eights tend to walk through the world with brick energy all the time, even when the situation calls for feather energy.

Brick energy is necessary and useful, just not in all situations. Often, people who experience Eights as "too much" want them to tone it down or to subdue their energy. But the work of the Eight isn't to do away with their energy; rather, it is to learn how to harness it from a grounded place. When the type structure is in the driver's seat, Eights are run by their brick energy and are often unaware that there might be another option for how to show up. When they practice building awareness and curiosity, they are more able to exercise choice in determining how much energy is suitable for the present moment.

Eights also have a sense that the world has harmed them unjustly, and so they organize their lives around exacting justice as a way to right this wrong. They are always on the lookout for injustice and are willing to use their strength and energy to fight for the underdog at the drop of a hat. Often, this is a subconscious attempt to seek restitution for the harm they themselves endured in their formative years. Acknowledging their own experiences of being harmed might bring up feelings of sadness, pain, or hurt. Since these softer feelings don't align with the story of strength, they subconsciously project their own experiences of harm onto all the underdogs they fight for, which allows them to show up as the person they needed when they were the underdogs themselves.

Also, because Eights are looking for injustice everywhere, they see it in places it might not even exist. They then bring their brick energy to smash windows in the name of justice, when a simple practice of pausing to collect themselves might show them that the situation is different than they initially perceived. This desire for vengeance and to right wrongs is what creates the mental habit of **revenge** in Eights, who can take the rather biblical eye-for-an-eye approach to justice.

AVOIDANCE

Weakness, Vulnerability

If you must be powerful and strong to protect yourself in a harsh world, then anything that is perceived as weakness or vulnerability is avoided at all costs. As we already explored, "soft" emotions like sadness, fear, or pain are considered weak to Eights. This type is most likely to meet sad or scary situations with a "toughen up" mantra that keeps Eights focused on being strong while ignoring their pain. They expend so much energy in keeping themselves hardened so as to not be perceived as weak.

The limitations of an Eight's body can also feel like weakness to them. Often, Eights push themselves without regard for their bodies' needs for rest and care. The need to slow down or practice self-care might be written off as weak and soft. When inevitably their bodies break down in a desperate cry for help, they are forced to reckon with an even greater vulnerability. Both within themselves and with the people around them, they avoid feeling inferior and incapable. On a deeper level, Eights fear that their greatest flaw is being weak, and in a world they believe seeks to overpower and harm, they must eradicate weakness in themselves completely in order to survive.

Not asking for help is one of the ways in which Eights avoid vulnerability. The rigid mantra of strength says, "*I can handle anything.*" Therefore, asking for help reeks of weakness and vulnerability to Eights. An Eight once told me a story of how he attempted to chop down a tree in his front yard using an axe because that was all he had. His neighbor, seeing how much energy it was taking to use an axe, offered his own chainsaw. This Eight was incredibly offended and immediately angry at the insinuation that he wasn't able to handle cutting down the tree without help, even though he was drenched in sweat and exhausted! Proving themselves as tough and able to withstand anything thrown at them means that Eights avoid admitting when they need help, or when their bodies need rest, no matter the cost.

I avoid vulnerability and weakness by putting forth a persona of having it all together. I don't show the fullness of my humanity to other people, which means that I'm not showing it to myself as well. Sometimes I have many things together but certainly not all the time, and I recently realized that people don't know this because I don't show them. Part of being vulnerable is actually being able to give people your heart and trust them with it in some way, and I don't do that. I've realized how internally armored I am. If my inner guard is up, then I don't have access to my vulnerability. It's locked in a tower somewhere.

On the outside, I'm happy Jessica with a big laugh and dimples who sings all the time. Maybe if I'm not singing or smiling or laughing as much you'd know something's up. But for the most part, it's really hard for people to tell because my armoring is so internal that I honestly don't even know sometimes when I'm being armored. When I am able to relax or I'm alone again, I look back and realize that I did not show up nearly as authentically as I thought I did. I can also easily get trapped into mistaking transparency for vulnerability. I can tell people I'm not doing well and they're like, "Well, we didn't know it was that bad." Me saying it out loud means it's true, but I often don't know how to show it because showing it would be a lot more vulnerable.

—Jessica Denise Dickson

Often, Eights believe an internal story that the harm and pain they experienced in their formative years were due to their own weakness or vulnerability. They were either made to feel weak by important people in their lives or might have even been blamed for things that were outside of their control as children. To ensure they never have to experience that sort of pain again, Eights work hard to eradicate all forms of weakness and vulnerability within themselves. They believe that if they are strong enough, they can avoid their core fear, which is of ending up **powerless** and being taken advantage of.

It makes sense to want to protect yourself if you have had experiences in which someone abused their power over you or took advantage of you when your defenses were down. And because Eights exist in the Body Center's binary approach to life, they come to believe that this is what will happen if they ever allow themselves to be vulnerable again. The desire to never experience that kind of pain is what fuels this avoidance of vulnerability in Eights.

I would describe the Nigerian culture I grew up in to be an Eight culture, in which you are expected to be loud and in charge, to never show vulnerability and weakness, and to make people pay if they hurt you. In many ways, this kind of armor is also expected from Black folks in the United States. The "strong Black woman" trope relies heavily on this kind of armoring, presenting a put-together, I-don't-need-no-body front to the world, like Jessica shares in her story. Having tough skin can certainly help us be more resilient in the face of ongoing threats to our well-being, but if we aren't intentional about creating space between our soft selves and the armor we carry, we run the risk of reducing our capacity to feel anything other than anger. We know that it is impossible to close yourself off to pain and vulnerability without also closing yourself off to joy. My favorite definition of vulnerability is a willingness to be affected by the world around us. Eights miss out on the innocent joy, love, and affection that is available to us when we are willing to be affected by the world.

> The fear of ending up powerless shows up like a freeze response in my body. I just don't move. I feel really rigid. If I feel like you're going to hurt me, I get numb hands and numb feet. I feel like I shouldn't move; I clench my gut and hold in my pelvic floor. Which is interesting as an Eight whose typical reaction is to jump into action. I put up all of the guarding that I need to really make sure that I'm safe, which sucks sometimes because I don't always know what I really need. I'm so practiced in putting up all of the armor that it's hard to know when I don't actually need it. Instead of taking off the armor, I make a power play. What do I need to do to make sure that there is some level of power that I have in this situation? Sometimes it's really subtle. Most of the time, the person doesn't even know that I've done it, but I've either cut something off or made sure that I'm the one who's in charge of something so that I have some semblance of control. It comes out really subtle, and I'm not usually conscious of it. The worst part is that it happens with the good stuff too. You try to protect yourself, to block out the bad stuff, but often it backfires. I still get hurt anyway. It's still not the outcome I want.
>
> —Jessica Denise Dickson

DEFENSE MECHANISM

Denial

Denial is the glue that holds this type structure together, making it such that Eights can uphold the story of rigid strength while denying their vulnerabilities. Denial can take on many forms for Eights, from denying their vulnerable feelings to denying their bodies' needs for rest and healing to denying their need for affection, affirmation, and acceptance. Denial also lends itself to the emotional habit of this type, which is **lust**. This lust isn't so much sexual as it is a constant, insatiable craving for more. Eights are lustful for more, for bigger and better in all things. Denying their own limitations or vulnerabilities fuels this habit of using their energy and passion to seek after more and more. They bring this big, lustful energy to everything they do, seeking intensity and excitement in order to feel alive.

Denial also makes Eights believe that the problem is outside of themselves: the world is a place where people are out to get you or treat you unjustly or take advantage of you. And, of course, if this is true of the world, then the hardened armor that the Eight carries is the only way to remain protected. In this way, denial shifts the attention from the Eight's own fears of powerlessness or their own experiences of pain to the badness or hardness of the world.

Denial protects the Eight's distorted and partial perception of reality and keeps the attention on hardening the armor of rigid strength. Of course, the world is filled with people who choose to take advantage of others and inflict harm. Pretending that isn't true would be another distortion of reality. But it is true that we tend to see what we are looking for. For the Eight, their lens of partial truth paints *everyone* into a potential enemy and the world into a battlefield in which there are only winners and losers. This makes it incredibly difficult to notice what else might be true. It often takes a monumental event to force an Eight to be present and honest with their own vulnerability. When an Eight is forced into a vulnerable position, like an injury or a medical diagnosis that forces them into accepting the help of others, they learn that people can show up with love and care in the face of their powerlessness. They can practice leaning into trusting others—a difficult learning process for Eights—when they begin to broaden their singular perception of truth.

If I didn't have to be strong all the time, my first thought is that I would be completely unprotected. And what would the point of that really be? But in reality, if I have access to more of who I am other than just my strength, I imagine that there would be more of an openness that I could actually show. I could trust that when I need my strength it will be there to really support me, and so I don't have to always be carrying the sword and shield or drawing a circle of fire around me so nothing else can get through. I imagine that I could give myself the permission to allow my heart to be touched by someone else.

My armor of strength feels the most necessary when I'm showing up in spaces where I feel like people expect me to be a certain way for them. I run my own business so that I can show up however I want. I think being able to create my life in that way has given me more space for true vulnerability. But it's often when I feel like I have to show up to be a certain way with people that I'm really guarded because I don't know what they're gonna ask of me, and I don't know if I really want to give it to them. So I stay guarded until I know that I don't need my guard up. When my guard's down, you'll get like the silly, ridiculous, Jessica, who sings and laughs and is six years old at heart. Until I know that that's okay, my guard stays up.

—Jessica Denise Dickson

CREATING SPACE BETWEEN SELF AND ARMOR

Notice—Pause—Allow

Remember that your practice is to notice, pause, and allow what comes up to be there without judgment or shame. Let compassion, gratitude, and curiosity guide you as you use the following prompts and exercises to practice bringing awareness to your experience of the type structure. Below are some helpful ways to begin noticing the patterns of your type. The stress and security movements and somatic profile can help you begin to practice curiosity when you notice yourself showing up in these ways.

Stress and Security Movements

When Eights are experiencing stress, they move toward Five. A conscious movement to Five can help Eights prioritize alone time to reflect and recharge. In the space of Five, they can pause from their typical march-forward-no-matter-what energy and detach enough to gain clarity before moving back into action. The unconscious movement to Five can present a challenge for Eights in that it is possible for them to become completely shut down, either detached from their bodies and emotions or overwhelmed by them.

When Eights are relaxed and feel secure, they move toward the space of the Two. A conscious movement to Two allows Eights to access more empathy and connection, for themselves and others. They have more ability to show up with a generosity of self that allows them to be vulnerable. The challenge with an unconscious movement toward Two is that Eights can feel overwhelmed by the vulnerable and tender emotions that they have for so long denied within themselves.

Somatic Profile

The body of an Eight holds a high amount of energy. Their action-oriented style is reflected in the way their bodies tend to lean forward whether sitting or standing. Their bodies, and muscles in particular, are often physically tense due to the habitual pattern of keeping out vulnerable needs or feelings. This pattern of armoring can deaden Eights' ability to fully experience the sensations of calm, relaxation or ease. Because of this, they get bored easily and impatiently leave the present moment in search of greater intensity that can penetrate their tough armor.

Journal Prompts

Below are some prompts to help you begin to practice curiosity around the story of your type. Find a quiet place to reflect on these questions. Remember to be present with your body as you answer these prompts. Notice, pause, and allow. Be compassionate, curious, and grateful to your body for its intelligence. You can come back to this practice as often as you need to.

1. What is your earliest memory of feeling joyful and free? Where were you? Who were you with? What were you doing? Pause to check in: How does your body feel right now as you write about it?
2. What would change about the way you live if it were true that showing up with childlike curiosity can help you reconnect with your own inherent goodness? Pause to check in: How does your body feel right now as you write about it?
3. What if it's true that you can be vulnerable and show weakness without losing worth or belonging?
4. If you didn't *have* to be strong all the time, who would you be free to be?
5. When is your armor of strength necessary in your everyday life? When is it *not* necessary?
6. What does safety feel like in your body? Who do you feel safe with, enough to set down the armor? How

does your body feel when you're with that person? Are you feeling some of that safety right now? You can always return to this space within yourself no matter what is happening outside of you.

Visualizations

Find a quiet place where you can relax without worry of interruption. If you are able, sit comfortably upright, uncrossing your hands and placing both feet flat on the floor. If you aren't able to do so, adjust your body to a position that helps you feel comfortable and grounded. Read through the prompt below, then close your eyes and begin to visualize. When you have completed the visualization, slowly bring your attention back to your body and the surface you are resting on, listen to the sounds around you, and open your eyes.

1. Visualize yourself picking up strength and putting it on like armor. What does your armor look like? How does your body feel when you are carrying the armor?
2. Visualize yourself taking off the armor of strength and setting it down. How does your body feel when you imagine setting down the armor in a safe space?

Community Practice

Often, we subconsciously weaponize our armor against others. If we live by a singular story, we try to subject others to that singular story as well. Because you believe you must be strong to have worth and belonging, you might require others around you to be strong in order to belong. Because you avoid your own vulnerability and weakness, you might detest or judge harshly others who appear weak to you. As you create space between yourself and your armor, I encourage you to consider how you require those around you to fit into your singular story. As you become more comfortable being with your own vulnerabilities and weaknesses, you will increase your capacity to be with other people's expressions of vulnerability and weakness.

Chapter 8

TYPE ONE: GOODNESS AS ARMOR

NICKNAMES	The Perfectionist, The Reformer
ARMOR	Goodness
HOLY IDEA	Perfection
VIRTUE/ESSENCE QUALITY	Serenity
MENTAL HABIT	Resentment
EMOTIONAL HABIT	Anger

HOLY IDEA

HOLY PERFECTION: The Sunset

Picture yourself sitting on a beach watching the sky's colors change as the sun begins its nightly disappearing act. Everywhere you look, the ever-changing colors are stunning as they shift from light orange to deep red to soft purple. You sit back and drink in the beauty, marveling at the perfection of the sunset—how the sun seems to grow bigger as it dips lower and lower toward the horizon, how the clouds soak up and disperse the light from the setting sun. This sunset is perfectly as it should be. Nothing is missing, and nothing needs to be changed to make it better. What the sky does on this particular evening is enough, and you enjoy it for what it is. And even though tomorrow's sunset will likely look much different, you will find yourself marveling at it once again, not comparing it to today's but letting it be exactly what it is.

This is a depiction of **Holy Perfection**, the objective reality, or Holy Idea, associated with the Type One structure. Holy Perfection is *a state of experiencing the undivided oneness and perfection that exists in all things in each moment*. As with every beautiful sunset, perfection can be found in each moment, as the light changes and the colors deepen. There is no golden standard for what a sunset should look like as each moment is so different as the light shifts. Life's invitation to us is to pause, notice, and enjoy what is unfolding before our eyes, allowing ourselves to witness the unfolding beauty for what it is without judgment. Since we understand that the sunset's unfolding happens outside of our control, we are free to simply appreciate it and be with it rather than attempt to modify it.

It would be futile to critique the sunset because you have no power to change it in any way. Meanwhile, the time and energy spent critiquing takes away from the ability to pause and notice what is lovely and already perfect about the sunset's unfolding. Yet this is exactly what happens when a One is disconnected from Holy Perfection. It is as though the One sits on the beach at sunset saying, "Now, if only the hues were a little darker over here, and if the purples could highlight these particular clouds over there, *then* this sunset would be perfect." The One overestimates their own sense of control and responsibility, and rather than answering the invitation to enjoy what is perfect as is, they spend their time trying to exert control to make life the way they think it *should* be.

When a One is connected to Holy Perfection, they exude the virtue of **serenity**. In describing this virtue, the Serenity Prayer is often referenced. The prayer, originally written by Reinhold Niebuhr and simplified and popularized by Alcoholics Anonymous, says, "God grant me the serenity to accept the things I cannot change, courage to change the things I can, and wisdom to know the difference." It is an apt description of the virtue we see in Ones when they remember that they have limited control over life's unfolding and allow themselves to accept—and find the already present perfection in—reality rather than stand against reality.

IDEALIZATION

Good, Right

When a One forgets that there is already perfection to be found in each moment, they create a subjective story that says that the world is a place in which we are constantly judged and punished for our bad behavior and impulses. If this story is true, then the only way to gain worthiness and

THE ENNEAGRAM FOR BLACK LIBERATION

belonging is to be good and act right. Ones hold themselves to incredibly high standards because they believe that it is their goodness that makes them worthy. They are constantly looking to become more perfect versions of themselves and to make more perfect versions of their lives and relationships.

Ones are naturally conscientious, responsible, and honest people. They are detail oriented, believe in doing things correctly, and bring their best to all their endeavors. They tend to be clear and direct communicators and are committed to living lives that match their ideals and values. When the type structure takes over, however, these characteristics are co-opted into maintaining a sense of goodness by constantly striving to get things right and to do the right thing. Ones become hypercritical of themselves, constantly monitoring and judging their behavior and responses against the scale of good versus bad. Since Ones are in the Body Center, they have the tendency to exist in only the binaries of good versus bad and right versus wrong. And because Ones believe that it is their behavior that makes them good or bad, there is a quick leap to a verdict of badness and wrongness when they make mistakes or make wrong decisions. There is no in-between. There is no room to consider that good people also make mistakes. The type structure's story is that to be good, you must be perfect and blameless. Ones have the loudest inner critic of all the types, and that critical voice is constantly reminding them of their flaws and how they continue to miss the mark of perfection.

> Being good means being the person that I intend to be and not the person that I am. It's being above reproach, criticism, or correction. It's never making a mistake or having to apologize for doing anything wrong.
>
> —Dayo

If the standard that Ones held themselves to were achievable, the fixation of the type structure might be productive. But when the standard is perfection, Ones are left struggling to attain the unattainable, and by doing so, they miss out on what is already perfect and good about who they are. We've all heard the phrase, "perfect is the enemy of good." This is incredibly true for Ones, whose desire to attain perfection makes it impossible for them to notice the goodness that already exists. This tendency toward criticism isn't just internal. Although Ones are more critical of themselves than anyone else, they are also critical of the external world, and others often experience them as super judgmental. Their attention naturally goes toward what could be improved in themselves, their environment, and the world at large. This can leave others they are in relationships with feeling as though they are never good enough. Of course, it is difficult for Ones to see others around them as good enough when they struggle with seeing themselves as good enough.

This preoccupation with being good and acting right leads to a mental habit of **resentment** in Ones. Since they spend so much of their energy on monitoring and controlling their behavior and impulses, Ones can feel resentful that other people aren't as conscientious as they are. To them, it feels like they are the only ones who really care about things getting done the right way, and they are likely to be the people who choose to do everything solo because they believe no one else will get it right. Resentment builds when their natural gift of responsibility morphs into a hyper-responsibility, especially for things that are outside of their control.

Like with the imagery of the sunset, Ones' attention immediately goes to what is wrong and needs to be fixed within themselves and in the world around them. The invitation, though, is to consider what is already right, good, and perfect within themselves and the world around them. We need the gift Ones bring in terms of challenging us all to keep improving. But when this gift gets disconnected from what is true and real, it becomes less of a gift and more of a burden. Imperfection is an inevitable part of being human, and it is our imperfections that create space within us to receive love, care, and kindness. The illusion of perfection acts as a shield that deflects all the goodness and love we would feel if only we allowed ourselves to be flawed and realize that we are still worthy.

AVOIDANCE

Being Wrong, Mistakes

Since Ones believe that they must be good and act right to have worth, they avoid being wrong, making mistakes, and even their own anger as a way to maintain the idealized story. In order to avoid being wrong, a One might delay action while anxiously triple-checking to make sure they got something right. Their emphasis on being conscientious and detail oriented is to avoid making a mistake or being wrong.

Ones are actually very sensitive to external criticism, even though it might appear that they dish it out to others without reserve. If so much of their identity is wrapped around being good, then criticism about their behavior threatens to topple that fragile internal system. To avoid the pain of criticism, Ones strive to make no mistakes and always act right. To do this, they engage in constant self-monitoring to make sure they are living up to this ideal of perfection. They tend to be rigid in both physical posture and internal belief system because they are working so hard to contain the "badness" within themselves and only allow the good out.

Since I'm a social Type One, I'm not as detail oriented or perfectionistic as other Type Ones, but because I already have the imprint of excellence and quality imbedded into my DNA, even some of my most sloppy works can appear like they have few or no imperfections. I don't try to avoid mistakes or being wrong. Unfortunately, I can't. So instead, I just allow myself to let my natural tendency to overcorrect and "do the most" take care of it. It works 90 percent of the time, but I only remember the 10 percent when things go terribly wrong and I can feel the criticism coming my way.

—Dayo

Ones also work hard to contain their anger because, in their binary view of the world, anger is bad. Good people don't get angry or make decisions out of anger, and so rather than being present with their anger and what meaningful truth it could be leading them to, they suppress it. Ones subconsciously believe that at their core, they are made up of badness and darkness. This is why they expend so much energy containing or suppressing their impulses and desires. They fear that giving in to those desires and impulses will open a trapdoor filled with all the horrible things that are true of them.

When I say desires or impulses, I am not referring to a desire to cheat on a partner, for example, or to harm someone else. Even innocent desires like to take a nap or to indulge in a pleasurable activity just for the sake of having fun can bring up this internal fear of opening the trapdoor. Ones tend to avoid pleasure because it might lead them to let their guard down and accidentally make a mistake or unleash the demons they believe are on the other side of the trapdoor. In the world of a One, it is much better to focus on being useful and responsible than to follow pleasure down the road of inevitable darkness.

The core fear with this type structure is of being so bad that you are deemed **worthless**. Belonging is one of the core themes of the Body Center, and Ones desperately want to belong. They believe that a person must be perfect in order to be worthy of belonging. This is why the type's energy is spent in the relentless pursuit of perfection. Ones have a hard time seeing and believing in their own inherent worthiness that isn't based on what choices they make or fail to make. This internal belief system is what keeps the "*I must be good and act right*" story going strong.

> The fear of being so bad I end up worthless shows up in depression, which I think I'm currently in right now. Depression for this Type One, Wing Two, social subtype, young Black woman looks like isolation. It looks like ruminating on past hurts and pains. It looks like blaming others for the state of my life. It looks like sleeping all day and binge-watching TV. When that fear of losing my worth because of my "badness" shows up, it looks like an overwhelming amount of sadness and willingly drowning in my emotions.
>
> —Dayo

DEFENSE MECHANISM

Reaction Formation

If you must be good and act right to be worthy of belonging, this means you must avoid making mistakes and being bad at all costs. The best way to do that is to constantly monitor yourself to preemptively catch any inklings of wrongness or badness and correct the impulse or reaction before it gets a chance to take hold. This constant monitoring and reforming of reactions is what we call reaction formation. Reaction formation is the pattern of repressing your impulses and reactions while acting in the opposite way.

Simply put, Ones are constantly internally judging their reactions as good or bad. When they categorize an internal reaction as "bad," they then quickly reform the reaction to something that keeps them safely in the "good" category. For example, a One might walk into a new friend's home and immediately think to herself, "Wow, this decor is not it." Then she internally reprimands herself for thinking such a "bad" thought about her new friend's home and seeks to reform it in a way that still maintains her sense of goodness. She says to her friend, "I love how your home is decorated!" This is the exact opposite of what the One actually feels! But reaction formation working swiftly in her subconscious gets her to overcorrect the supposed "bad" reaction for the opposite "good" one.

Every time I use this example to illustrate reaction formation to a One, I inevitably hear, "But what was she supposed to do? It's rude to tell someone you hate how their house is decorated!" It *is* rude because it's not your house and no one asked for your opinion. But this reaction highlights the One's (and all Body types') tendency to live in the binary of good and bad, right and wrong. To correct for the bad reaction, a good response must be offered. There is so much space that is missed between what is deemed good and bad, though. For example, a neutral response could look like: *"It's so good to see you! How are you?"* With this response, the One in my example could practice allowing herself to have a reaction to the space without labeling it as good or bad, and then she could carry on with her friend.

As is true for all the types, the defense mechanism works subconsciously, which makes it tricky to catch in action. Ones, who are deeply invested in being good and honest people, aren't aware of how often they morph their responses to fit in the category of good rather than allowing for what is true to simply be true. The emotional habit of Ones is **anger**, even though the type structure works hard to contain the anger or reform it into what the One thinks it should be. Ones are angry at all that is imperfect in themselves, their relationships, and the world, *and* they're angry at everyone else for not putting in more effort to correct the bad. Because this anger isn't given the space to be released, it is held within the body of the One and hardens into resentment and rigidity.

For any of you who were raised in the Christian church, this type structure might feel very familiar, even if it isn't your own home base. I think of Christianity as peak One culture. There is the binary of good and bad, a belief that at everyone's core is a mass of badness, and clear instructions on what to do or believe to become good and therefore worthy. Or there is the belief that nothing a person does makes them worthy, and only the right set of beliefs can do that. Even in a religion that holds the love of God as the underlying foundation, people are often judged harshly for their behavior and can come to believe that their worth comes from what they do or abstain from doing. Often being a good Christian requires employing the defense mechanism of reaction formation—constantly monitoring yourself to make sure nothing bad or wrong escapes your lips. No matter what type is home base, if you were raised in the Christian tradition, there is probably an overlay of Oneness that seeps through. The work of the One, then, is also for you.

If I didn't have to be good all the time, I would be free to be fun and spontaneous. It would honestly free me up to be selfish as well. Good people are selfless and give of themselves in ways that they probably shouldn't. They are responsible and never do anything that could potentially be seen as wrong, but if I didn't have to be good all the time, I would be fun. I would take trips out of the country. I would be irresponsible with my time and money. I would say no a lot more.

My armor of goodness is necessary when I'm trying to create and produce quality work and content. It's necessary when everyone around me is looking out for self instead of practicing selflessness. It's necessary when fighting injustice and giving advice. It's not necessary when I'm with God, who is fully aware of my badness and still chooses to be with me. It's not necessary when I'm with friends, who are safe spaces for me to show up as fully myself. It's not necessary when I'm having fun or trying to enjoy myself. In these times, it really doesn't matter if I'm good or bad. It just matters that I exist and that I get to participate in this gift called life with no fear or trying to measure up to some unattainable standard of perfection.

—Dayo

CREATING SPACE BETWEEN SELF AND ARMOR

Notice—Pause—Allow

Remember that your practice is to notice, pause, and allow what comes up to be there without judgment or shame. Let compassion, gratitude, and curiosity guide you as you use the following prompts and exercises to practice bringing awareness to your experience of the type structure. Below are some helpful ways to begin noticing the patterns of your type. The stress and security movements and somatic profile can help you begin to practice curiosity when you notice yourself showing up in these ways.

Stress and Security Movements

When Ones are experiencing stress, they move toward Four. A conscious movement to Four can help Ones allow themselves to express the emotions they typically suppress. This could be directly or through a creative outlet. Being in the Four space offers Ones the opportunity to practice making room for their emotions. The unconscious movement to Four can present a challenge for Ones in that, without consciousness, these suppressed feelings might erupt or explode in ways that are hurtful to others, or Ones might become overwhelmed by feelings of sadness and depression.

When Ones are relaxed and feel secure, they move toward the space of the Seven. A conscious movement to Seven allows Ones to be open, go with the flow, and have fun. They are able to explore multiple options and possibilities with enthusiasm. The challenge with an unconscious movement toward Seven is that with less rigidity and inhibition, Ones can swing to the other extreme and overindulge or act out.

Somatic Profile

Ones have a lot of physical energy, which they restrict in order to maintain control over their impulses and their feelings. This restriction creates rigidity and tension in their bodies, particularly around the neck, shoulders, jaw, diaphragm, and pelvic floor. It's almost as if they keep their bodies tense and rigid to ensure the "bad" doesn't leak out.

Journal Prompts

Below are some prompts to help you begin to practice curiosity around the story of your type. Find a quiet place to reflect on these questions. Remember to be present with your body as you answer these prompts. Notice, pause, and allow. Be compassionate, curious, and grateful to your body for its intelligence. You can come back to this practice as often as you need to.

1. What is your earliest memory of feeling joyful and free? Where were you? Who were you with? What were you doing? Pause to check in: How does your body feel right now as you write about it?
2. What would change about the way you live if it were true that your imperfection doesn't change your inherent goodness? Pause to check in: How does your body feel right now as you write about it?

3. What if it's true that you can be wrong and make mistakes without losing worth or belonging?
4. If you didn't *have* to be good all the time, who would you be free to be?
5. When is your armor of goodness necessary in your everyday life? When is it *not* necessary?
6. What does safety feel like in your body? Who do you feel safe with, enough to set down the armor? How does your body feel when you're with that person? Are you feeling some of that safety right now? You can always return to this space within yourself no matter what is happening outside of you.

Visualizations

Find a quiet place where you can relax without worry of interruption. If you are able, sit comfortably upright, uncrossing your hands and placing both feet flat on the floor. If you aren't able to do so, adjust your body to a position that helps you feel comfortable and grounded. Read through the prompt below, then close your eyes and begin to visualize. When you have completed the visualization, slowly bring your attention back to your body and the surface you are resting on, listen to the sounds around you, and open your eyes.

1. Visualize yourself picking up goodness and putting it on like armor. What does your armor look like? How does your body feel when you are carrying the armor?

2. Visualize yourself taking off the armor of goodness and setting it down. How does your body feel when you imagine setting down the armor in a safe space?

Community Practice

Often, we subconsciously weaponize our armor against others. If we live by a singular story, we try to subject others to that singular story as well. Because you believe you must be good to have worth and belonging, you might require others around you to adhere to your standard of goodness in order to belong. Because you avoid your own mistakes, you might detest or judge harshly the mistakes of others. As you create space between yourself and your armor, I encourage you to consider how you require those around you to fit into your singular story. As you become more comfortable being with your own mistakes and imperfection, you will increase your capacity to be with other people's mistakes and imperfection without judgment.

Chapter 9

THE HEART CENTER

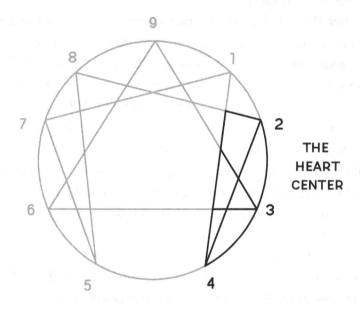

THE HEART CENTER

The Heart Center of intelligence is the seat of our emotional and relational wisdom. Heart types use their hearts to ensure that they remain in good relational standing with the people in their lives. Being seen in a positive light for who they are and what they do is central to this triad. To this end, they create images based on what they believe will help important others see them as deserving of love.

The core story with Heart types says that being who they are is not enough to be loved; they must *do* something to earn their relational keep. These types are often subconsciously wondering: *"Have I done enough to convince you that I am deserving of love?"* The image creation, then, is born from that story that they have to work hard to present images that earn them love because who they are at their cores is not enough.

For Black folks whose appearance is always subject to critique, this story can ring very true. When we are required to wear our hair a certain way to be considered "professional" in the workplace, we are creating and presenting an image to help us gain a type of acceptance. When we dress up to go shopping at certain stores to look like we have enough money to be there and avoid being followed by the store clerks, we are creating and presenting an image to gain acceptance. Often, for us, this is necessary armoring in a society that tells us we don't matter just as we are and that we must prove that our humanity is deserving of the same care and acceptance others get without question. This is what I believe is at the heart of asserting that Black lives matter—reminding ourselves and the world that we do not need to be anything other than who we are to be deserving of care, acceptance, and love.

Type Twos, Threes, and Fours use their hearts as an instrument of perception, particularly attuned to changes in connection with others. The heart is always measuring: *How am I in relation to you? How close or far do I feel from you?* Based on the perception of connection or disconnection, a lot of emotion can arise from this internal analysis–sadness, fear, or shame.

The core needs for Heart types are for **love**, approval, affection, connection, and appreciation. All of these needs are relational and connected to this triad's need to be seen positively in the eyes of others. Heart types tend to play whatever role is necessary to keep the connection and maintain approval. This means that all three types in this triad may struggle with authenticity, as they are more interested in approval and connection than in telling the full truth of who they are.

When the core needs are threatened, the emotions that arise are panic, shame, and grief. When your sense of self is tied to others' perception of you, there is a real sense of panic if that external perception is negative because it threatens your perceived access to love and approval. Shame also arises quickly when these needs are threatened because, as mentioned above, there is an underlying story of not-enoughness with the Heart Center. The story asserts that what is good and lovable about the person is the image, and without the image, there is nothing worthy of being seen, cherished, and loved. And when so much effort and energy is spent creating and polishing an image, it can become easy to confuse the image for who you are and lose contact with the self. However, on a deeper level, there *is* some consciousness around the loss of connection with the essential self, and this awareness can bring up grief for Heart types navigating the disconnection they feel from their own real selves.

Twos create an image of being helpful and generous, Threes of being successful and capable, and Fours of being interesting and authentic. Comparison shows up very clearly in this triad—Twos subconsciously want to believe they are more helpful than others, Threes better at achieving than others, and Fours more interesting than or different from others.

When Heart Center types are able to come home to who they truly are and remember their inherent value and loveliness, they are able to let themselves simply *be* without having to do anything to prove their enoughness. They are also able to value their own connection to self and hold affection and appreciation for self without it needing to be confirmed from the outside world.

Chapter 10

TYPE THREE: SUCCESS AS ARMOR

NICKNAMES	The Performer, The Achiever
ARMOR	Success
HOLY IDEA	Hope
VIRTUE/ESSENCE QUALITY	Veracity
MENTAL HABIT	Vanity/Motion
EMOTIONAL HABIT	Deceit

HOLY IDEA

HOLY HOPE: The Ocean Wave

Imagine you are sitting on the sandy shores of a beach, watching wave after wave roll in, crash, and recede into the vast ocean. The ocean is constantly in motion, and the waves move that energy from one area to another. Each wave seems distinct from the others, with its own swelling and rising and crashing. And at the same time, each wave also appears indistinct from the other waves, as they build on one another, rising and falling in tempo. Whether a tiny wave or a massive one, all are held inside of the expansiveness of the ocean. It would be impossible to extricate a single wave from the ocean that formed it. The job of a wave is simply to be a wave—a part of a grander system in motion—without trying to become the entire ocean.

Now, imagine that a singular wave attempts to carry the burden of cresting and crashing onto the entire shoreline. Maybe this wave believes that it can do the job better and more efficiently than all the other waves, and takes on the responsibility for something that was never its job in the first place. This wave forgets that while it is powerful and capable on its own, like every other wave, it, too, must recede back into the support of the vastness of the ocean. There is something much greater than the individual wave that, when this wave surrenders to it, allows for a beautiful synergy that gets the work done. When the wave remembers that it can lean on the strength of the ocean, that it is a part of this ocean, then it can focus on its own work knowing that the ocean provides the energy and resources for others to do their work as well.

This is a depiction of **Holy Hope**, the objective reality, or Holy Idea, associated with the Type Three structure. Holy Hope states that *things get done and work according to a universal law that is not dependent on an individual's effort*. This law is what sets—and keeps—things in motion and determines what truly needs to be accomplished and what amount of effort is necessary for the work. When we remember that the world isn't kept in motion by our individual doing, we have more capacity to experience hope. Holy Hope is a state of being in which we recognize that we are connected to and supported by something bigger than ourselves, which then frees us to focus on just what is ours to do. It is not the individual wave's effort that keeps the ocean in motion.

Freed from the belief that we have to be everything to everyone, or from the story that it is our continued effort that earns us value and love, we can focus on what our work is with joy and with hope because we don't need to prove anything by how hard we work. There is, of course, still work that gets done, but when we no longer believe that nothing moves until we do, there is more space for us to just *be*, to relax into the present moment. In that space, we remember that our value and lovability isn't tied to how much we produce and achieve. The word used to describe this quality of being is **veracity**, which simply means to habitually tell the truth about who you are. There is no need for image management when we believe that who we are is enough and deserving of love without effort. Veracity means a Three is able to show up honestly, without performance, bringing both their strengths and limitations, successes and failures, as part of their experience but not their entire identity.

IDEALIZATION

Successful, Capable, Competent

When a Three loses contact with Holy Hope, they become convinced that it *is* their individual effort that sustains the world around them. They work hard to become success-ful, and when they notice that their drive for success is applauded and celebrated, it starts to harden into armor. They begin to believe that they are only worthy of attention and love when they are seen as successful. They see their value as something external to them, something that others can decide based on what the Three proves they are capa-ble of achieving.

Threes are impressive people. They tend to come across as charming, personable, industrious, competitive, and fast paced. They are most likely at the helm of multiple projects at once and somehow manage to excel at all of them. They are master problem solvers who are able to look at obstacles in the way of a goal and find ways around and over those obstacles. They tend to be more focused on tasks over peo-ple which can often get them in trouble relationally. In fact, Threes can turn their relationships into yet another to-do list, prioritizing efficiency over being fully present to those around them.

Threes want to win no matter what, which means they are pros at shape-shifting, adjusting and managing their images to fit whatever is expected of them in that moment. If a Three walked into a social setting in which an intellec-tual debate was in motion, subconsciously they would put on their "Successful Intellectual" hat and amaze everyone in the room with their intelligence. But if the room was engaged in lighthearted banter, they would subconsciously put on their "Successful Comedian" hat and leave everyone clutching their sides trying to breathe. If they needed you to see them as a successful business owner, they would put on that hat. If they needed you to see them as a successful mother of three, they would put on that hat. While it could seem manipulative or superficial, being able to adapt their image easily to make a connection is really the superpower of the Three type structure. The intent here isn't for Threes to manipulate but to keep themselves safe from pain by ensuring they are constantly seen in a positive light for who they are and what they do.

The approval of others is one of the driving forces of the Three type structure, but it matters who the approval comes from. Not everyone's approval carries weight. People who are most important to the Three—those whose approval they fear losing the most—are the ones Threes unconsciously customize their armor to impress. This is where the stereotype about all Threes being high-powered CEOs motivated by money misses the heart of this type structure. Success for a Three is often defined by the important people in their life. If a Three wants to make their parents proud and the way to do so is by becoming a top litigator, that's what they will become. If the person whose approval they seek is impressed by people who have elaborate, thriving gardens, this Three will become a master gardener *and* make it look easy. The common denominator here is the belief that it is your doing that makes you valuable and earns you approval. Whether the doing looks like running your own company or cultivating the best garden in the neighborhood, the story of the Three convinces you that being impressive is the route to acceptance and love.

To maintain this story, Threes develop a mental habit of both **vanity** and constant **motion**. Vanity speaks to the habit of image management—making sure you always put your best foot forward, making sure you're always showing up in the way that is expected of you in order to make a good impression, shape-shifting to gain approval. Motion speaks to Threes' ability to live in go mode constantly, which serves to keep them from being fully present with themselves. If you're constantly in motion, you can choose to remain laser focused on your goals while ignoring anything else that might feel vulnerable or require you to stop doing long enough to check in with yourself.

> I am always thinking: At the end of my life, when my job is done, what does that look like? It looks like people's lives being better because of me. In my vision of my life well lived, I see myself as an instrument in the positive unfoldment and expansion of other people's purpose, happiness, and ability to create the life they want. That's what being successful means to me.
>
> —Danielle Fanfair

AVOIDANCE

Failure, Feelings

If your story says that you have to be seen as successful in order to be accepted and loved, failure will feel like a threat to that sense of love and acceptance and must be avoided at all costs. One of the ways people in the Three type structure work to avoid failure is by only attempting or engaging in things they are already good at. The goal is to win, and so Threes often will pick activities, hobbies, or events in which there is a low risk for them to fail.

Another way this type tries to avoid failure is through reframing it as a "learning opportunity." Rather than admitting that an attempt to start a company with a friend ended in failure, for example, a Three would more likely describe that experience as, "Not the best, but I learned a lot and came out so much better on the other side." Or say, "The lessons I learned from that experience helped me build this business I have today, so ultimately, that wasn't a failure because it really helped me succeed at the end of the day." While it is true that we can learn from our failures and grow, Threes rarely allow themselves to feel the necessary grief, frustration, or even weariness after something they worked hard for doesn't succeed. An important part of healing is being willing to sit with the difficult emotions that our experiences bring up. Often, the quick jump to reframing a difficult experience as a learning opportunity is an attempt to bypass the unresolved emotional pain and quickly return to using productivity as a weapon against vulnerability.

My Enneagram type kicks in when I feel myself falling into my fear of being a "bad" person, in whatever context. I have cultivated a habit of self-care when I start to hear my alarm clocks going off: irrational anger, frustration, and withdrawing into my own space. When those things are happening for me, I am able to notice, give myself what I need, and pivot my energy toward success.

—Danielle Fanfair

Vulnerable feelings are another thing Threes try to avoid. Feelings can be seen as obstacles that get in the way of accomplishing a goal. Remember that a part of the mental habit of a Three is to constantly be in motion, and attending to our feelings often requires that we slow down and pay attention. Slowing down doesn't come naturally to Threes, and especially not for feelings. If paying attention to a feeling that arises means that a Three can move closer to their goal, then being present with the feeling might be seen as a productive use of time. Otherwise, it is considered a nuisance. This pattern of avoidance also serves to protect Threes from the grief that can arise when they allow themselves to be still—grief around the loss of contact with who they truly are. On some level, Threes hold awareness that they are no longer sure who they are or if there really is someone worth seeing behind all the doing. To avoid the grief this awareness brings, they just keep moving.

The experience of failure is so devastating for Threes because there is no separation between who they are and what they do. If you are only worthy of love and acceptance when you do something successfully, then of course it feels devastating to fail. In fact, the core fear of a Three is just that–**being a total failure**. Being a failure means you lose access to connection, love, acceptance, and value. It makes sense that the type structure would try to protect against that kind of loss, but not every compelling story is a true story. While failure is uncomfortable and can truly be painful, failing at something is not a reflection of the fullness of your worth and value. It is possible to fail at achieving a goal and still be loved. It is possible to fail and be able to look that failure squarely in the face without making it about your value or lovability. But for a Three, it takes conscious work to be able to remember and believe this.

When my fear of being a failure is activated, my inner critic gets loud and tells me that everything I am doing is wrong, that any time not spent on actual work is wasted, and that I am just bad at the core and can't hide it anymore.

In my body, I feel these waves of anger and anxiety together, coursing up from my gut and then into my head where my thoughts and fears swirl around like indecipherable code. In my desperation to understand the code, I start to get very tired and irritable. Then, I project the energy out subconsciously, slamming things, bumping into things, sighing and rolling my eyes, and answering with a hard "*What?!*" when anyone calls me.

—Danielle Fanfair

DEFENSE MECHANISM

Identification

The defense mechanism that keeps this type structure going is called identification, which refers to the Three's subconscious overidentification with the roles they play in a way that leads to a loss of contact with the true self. If a Three plays the role of mother, partner, and CEO, the type structure tells her that she must perform excellently in all three of those roles to be seen as deserving of love and acceptance. Identification keeps her from her avoidance by melding her sense of identity with what she does, making it such that any win or failure feels deeply personal. If she wins, it means she is loved and valuable. If she fails, it means she isn't worth being kept around. After years of this, it can be difficult to know if there is anything worth loving about her beyond what she does and how well she shows up in those roles.

In this way, a Three becomes an expert at **deceit**, which is the emotional habit of the type structure. This deceit is less about consciously deceiving others and more about the self-deceit required to maintain an image of who you should be at the expense of who you truly are. Threes deceive themselves into believing they are the roles they play, and they distance themselves from anything else that might be true of them.

If you are constantly stepping into roles and confusing your identity with what you do, losing yourself in the doing becomes easy, but it doesn't offer you freedom. There will never be a point you reach where the doing is satisfied and you can allow yourself to simply be. When one goal is attained, a new goal is set. If your identity is wrapped up in being successful at the roles you play, then all your effort only serves to polish the prison—not walk out of it.

As mentioned in an earlier chapter, the United States is often referred to as a Type Three culture. We can see this narrative about success, image management, and approval everywhere we look. Collectively, the "person" we're trying to impress is our capitalist system, and its definition for success is very limited: amassing and hoarding wealth, and likability as a requirement to earn social capital. We all know that when we are working really hard to be liked, we are often not telling the full truth of who we are and what we need, both to ourselves and to those around us. And the more we do this, the easier it becomes to forget who we really are and to attach our identities to these likable images we've created for others to consume. The easiest example of this is social media. Instagram is a master class in image management and likability. The actual definition of success on that platform is gauged by how many people like and engage with you and the "brand" you've created! To continue to be successful, you must keep fine-tuning and polishing that image until it sparkles, even if it isn't true to who you are anymore. No matter what Enneagram type is home base for you, if you live in the United States, there is an overlay of Three-ness injected into your armor. It is the way we are socialized to survive and gain acceptance in this culture.

If I didn't have to be successful all the time, I'd be the person who cultivates functional, meaningful fun all the time. I'd produce festivals, DJ the after-parties, and always be somewhere swimming.

I am a Black woman—knowing the rules and behaving in a way that is appropriate and correct I am *sure* has saved my life. So I see where my ability to scan the environment and govern myself with discernment and discipline comes in handy, especially in privileged spaces and spaces that are not safe for me.

The armor of success is not necessary when I have friends and family who love me for me and are waiting for me to relax. My energy is so strong that it permeates whatever environment I choose to enter. When I am serene and moving according to the perfect vision that I have for my life, everything falls into place better than I can arrange it. I don't need the armor because there is no battle there.

—Danielle Fanfair

CREATING SPACE BETWEEN SELF AND ARMOR

Notice—Pause—Allow

Remember that your practice is to notice, pause, and allow what comes up to be there without judgment or shame. Let compassion, gratitude, and curiosity guide you as you use the following prompts and exercises to practice bringing awareness to your experience of the type structure. Below are some helpful ways to begin noticing the patterns of your type. The stress and security movements and somatic profile can help you begin to practice curiosity when you notice yourself showing up in these ways.

Stress and Security Movements

When Threes are experiencing stress, they move toward Nine. A conscious movement to Nine can help Threes soften their naturally competitive nature. In the Nine space, Threes can become more inclusive, able to seek out more viewpoints instead of just their own. Threes might also be able to access a slower rhythm of life, prioritizing rest and care rather than being in constant motion. The unconscious movement to Nine can result in a Three having difficulty paying attention or the Three becoming stuck in laziness, passivity, or inactivity.

When Threes are relaxed and feel secure, they move toward the space of the Six. A conscious movement to Six gives Threes the space to bring attention to the aspects of their lives often overlooked in their quest for success and forward motion. In the space of the Six, they are able to think about their relationships and lives in a nonperformative way. The challenge with an unconscious movement toward Six is that a Three might feel distressed by the unfamiliar anxiety and fear that can arise, especially when the Three's constant motion is paused.

Somatic Profile

Threes have a high body charge, and a lot of that energy is held in their chest area. Because of their high energy, sitting still is difficult for Threes, and they instead focus on action and productivity as a way to discharge the energy. Since they tend to avoid being with their own feelings, tension might build up around their heart area from the unexplored emotions, most especially grief. It is said that this pattern of armoring over their hearts may make them more vulnerable to early heart attacks or a weakened immune system.

Journal Prompts

Below are some prompts to help you begin to practice curiosity around the story of your type. Find a quiet place to reflect on these questions. Remember to be present with your body as you answer these prompts. Notice, pause, and allow. Be compassionate, curious, and grateful to your body for its intelligence. You can come back to this practice as often as you need to.

1. What is your earliest memory of feeling joyful and free? Where were you? Who were you with? What were you doing? Pause to check in: How does your body feel right now as you write about it?
2. What would change about the way you live if it were true that you don't need to earn value or love by being seen as successful or accomplished? Pause to check in: How does your body feel right now as you write about it?
3. What if it's true that you can fail at everything you do and still be deserving of acceptance and love?

4. If you didn't *have* to be successful all the time, who would you be free to be?
5. When is your armor of success necessary in your everyday life? When is it *not* necessary?
6. What does safety feel like in your body? Who do you feel safe with, enough to set down the armor? How does your body feel when you're with that person? Are you feeling some of that safety right now? You can always return to this space within yourself no matter what is happening outside of you.

Visualizations

Find a quiet place where you can relax without worry of interruption. If you are able, sit comfortably upright, uncrossing your hands and placing both feet flat on the floor. If you aren't able to do so, adjust your body to a position that helps you feel comfortable and grounded. Read through the prompt below, then close your eyes and begin to visualize. When you have completed the visualization, slowly bring your attention back to your body and the surface you are resting on, listen to the sounds around you, and open your eyes.

1. Visualize yourself picking up success and putting it on like armor. What does your armor look like? How does your body feel when you are carrying the armor?
2. Visualize yourself taking off the armor of success and setting it down. How does your body feel when you imagine setting down the armor in a safe space?

Community Practice

Often, we subconsciously weaponize our armor against others. If we live by a singular story, we try to subject others to that singular story as well. Because you believe you must be seen as successful to have value and be loved, you might dismiss others who don't applaud your performance. Because you avoid your own failure, you might be intolerant of the failures of others. As you create space between yourself and your armor, I encourage you to consider how you require those around you to fit into your singular story. As you become more comfortable being with your own experiences of failure as separate from your inherent value, you will increase your capacity to be with other people's failures as well.

Chapter 11

TYPE TWO: HELPFULNESS AS ARMOR

NICKNAMES	The Giver, The Helper
ARMOR	Helpfulness
HOLY IDEA	Freedom
VIRTUE/ESSENCE QUALITY	Humility
MENTAL HABIT	Flattery
EMOTIONAL HABIT	Pride

HOLY IDEA

HOLY FREEDOM: The River

Let's imagine that you live within a small community of people without indoor plumbing. To wash their clothes and cook their meals, they rely on water from a nearby river. The river brings in fresh water, cool and crisp on a hot day, and pure enough to drink straight from the source. There is no muddiness, nor are there bacterial strains lurking in these waters, and the river sustains the lives and livelihoods of you and your community members. No one can really tell where this river flows from and where it goes. But it has never once run dry and has a constant flow of fresh water available whenever anyone needs it. When your reserves of water are depleted at home, all you have to do is go down to the river and fill your containers back up. This is the repetitive cycle: you recognize you have a need, you honor the need by going to the river and letting it replenish you, you use that replenishment to sustain your life until the need emerges again. The river is always available to everyone; its invitation is for you to listen to your thirst and come get replenished as many times as you need to.

This is a depiction of **Holy Freedom**, the objective reality, or Holy Idea, associated with the Type Two structure. Holy Freedom is a deep knowing that *there is a universal will that satisfies and meets all real needs, which then allows us to experience the freedom to honor our own needs and seek replenishment.* Holy Freedom reminds us that part of being human is being needy, and it is our neediness that increases our capacity to receive love. If we pretend we have no needs, we close ourselves off to the love and care that would otherwise be available to us.

When someone with the Two type structure becomes disconnected from this objective reality, they begin to weave a subjective story, one that says that *they* are the river that sustains the community. Rather than tend to their own needs like the river invites everyone to do, they spend more time checking for and responding to their neighbors' needs. They might spend the entirety of their day pouring water from their own reserves into their neighbors' containers, not once stopping to recognize that they themselves are parched and in desperate need of water. Obviously, this isn't sustainable because without water they will die. But they give and give of their own reserves, silently hoping others will take notice of how hard they are working to sustain the community and begin to take care of them too.

However, Holy Freedom reminds the Two that single-handedly sustaining the community was never their work and invites the Two to embrace the freedom of neediness, just like everyone else. When Twos begin to see themselves as just as in need of replenishment as everyone else, they begin to embody the virtue of **humility**. Humility allows them to see themselves rightly—with neither an inflated sense of being needed nor a deflation of their own needs. Humility allows them to respond to real needs, theirs and those of others around them, without conflating being of service with earning love and approval.

IDEALIZATION

Helpful, Generous

As we've seen already, the story of the Two is that they *must* be seen as helpful and generous by those around them and especially those who are important to them. All Heart types (Twos, Threes, and Fours) create images that help them to be seen in a positive light for the purpose of earning love, connection, and approval. Twos believe they must be helpful in order to be loved. In other words, they must give love to get love.

Twos are naturally kind, empathic, nurturing, generous people. Their superpower is being able to sense what others need and respond to that need without hesitation. They are friendly and open and tend to focus most of their energy on others. At their best, Twos know how to make people feel seen and loved. They are naturally positive people who see the best in others and in the world around them and genuinely want to support and encourage others. However, to be seen in a positive light and maintain connection with others, they develop the mental habit of **flattery**. They tend to overpraise and exaggerate their positive feelings toward others as a way to remain liked and not lose out on connection. While naming what we love and admire about others is a good practice, flattery is an insincere form of praise that serves to further personal interests. In this case, the personal interest is ensuring that the Two remains in good relational standing with the person they are flattering.

Women are generally socialized to look like Twos to be acceptable. The natural nurturing, helpful caretaking characteristics that are second nature to the Two are held up as the ideal of how women should be. Because of that, many women mistype as Twos when they first encounter the Enneagram since it is who we are told we must be.

One of the major difficulties of the Type Two structure is the tendency to conflate being helpful with being deserving of love. Twos have a deep need to be needed because they believe that if they aren't indispensable in people's lives, they will be replaced. What happens, then, if you believe you have to constantly be satisfying the other person's needs to keep a relationship afloat? You might begin to manufacture needs in order to have something to do.

Doing to earn love is a common theme across the Heart Center. It is important to note here that most of the time, this helper energy isn't just directed at anyone a Two meets. It is usually reserved for their circle of important people, whether that's family, close friends, work friends, and so on. If a Two is partnered with someone who leans more toward self-sufficiency, they might create needs to meet as a way to alleviate their internal sense of panic or distress around becoming disposable. In this way, Twos' helpfulness can sometimes be experienced as intense and intrusive by the people in their lives. The energy with which this helpfulness comes across is not one that is grounded in the deep knowing that they are already worthy of love but one that is a little panicky, one that says, *"Please let me love and take care of you so you never leave me!"* Other people can sense that energy and might feel manipulated by the Two's helpfulness. They might feel, and rightfully so, as though the Two is only giving to get.

Twos have one of the highest views of self across the types. They truly believe themselves to be good, selfless, wonderful people. They absolutely are. And yet part of growth and healing requires looking at the ways in which the images we've created of ourselves are disconnected from reality. Because Twos think of themselves as selfless and generous, it is hard for them to see that their constant giving might often have more to do with them and less with the people on the receiving end. It is really painful for Twos to admit—after years of thinking of themselves as selfless—that they are actually more motivated by their own self-interests. Giving to avoid the pain of rejection or disapproval isn't selfless giving. However, it is a response that makes sense to all of us as humans because in our own different ways we organize ourselves and our lives around the avoidance of pain.

Here's the thing: those in relationships with Twos are already aware that the Two in their life is human. By human, what I mean is complicated, wonderful, messy, open-hearted, needy, selfish, endearing, generous—the whole range. So for a Two, rather than letting the recognition that you're not always selfless bring up shame, allow it to widen your capacity to be compassionate toward yourself and to receive compassion from others.

One of the ways that I've learned to approach helping other people and supporting other people is to really hold space to listen to what they have to share and what they need. I think sometimes the tendency for Type Twos can really be to jump to do something, and sometimes all people need is just someone to listen and someone to say, "Wow, you're seen and you're heard in this way." I think that is me at my best. And as I've grown, I've really seen helping other people as not trying to anticipate other people's needs as much as responding within my specific capacity to do so. I try to ask myself, "Why am I doing this? Do I have the capacity to do this? And if I can't help, who are some other people or resources I can connect them to?" I've realized that the way that I prefer to help is without obligation, but truly from this abundance of who I am and from a place in me that is full.

I think at my worst, help became like an obligation when I didn't have great boundaries. Being truly helpful is being boundaried. It's helping from a place of capacity, from a place that acknowledges that I'm not always the best person to help and can point people to what they need. It's holding space for other people without assuming I know best or I know what they need.

—Faye

AVOIDANCE

Their Own Needs, Disappointing Others

If your story says that you have to be seen as helpful in order to be accepted and loved, then being seen as needy is categorized as a threat to your love and connection. For Twos, letting others show up for them and take care of or support them can feel incredibly uncomfortable. Even though they spend so much of their time caring for the needs of others and crave appreciation for what they do, they are usually uncomfortable being in the spotlight. Having someone else notice a need and offer support upends the carefully erected system that places the Two in the permanent position of giver and everyone else in the permanent position of receiver. When so much energy is spent in the posture of giving, receiving becomes difficult.

It is impossible to be needless by virtue of being human. The pretense can only go so long before a basic human need—to use the bathroom or feed your hunger, for example—interrupts the game of pretend. Twos are often aware of their own needs, but rather than proactively meet those needs, they employ a variety of tactics to ignore or demote them. For example, let's say a Two is teaching a workshop for a small group of people and notices that they need to pause for a bathroom break. When the type structure is firing on autopilot, they might seek group consensus as a way to garner permission to take care of their need. This could look like asking the whole group if anyone needs a bathroom break at that point, and if people opt in, the Two doesn't have to feel like their own need is taking center stage. Now that it's a collective need, the Two can play the role of helping the group feel cared for *and* also get their own need met. But remember that all of this began with the Two's need, which was then displaced onto the group. Another example of this is a Two who experiences hunger but feels like they aren't allowed to satiate their hunger without also feeding the people around them. They might offer to feed everyone in what is really an effort to satisfy their own hunger.

I don't feel like I actively avoid being needy. In a less healthy place, I would minimize my needs by centering other people above me. I wouldn't ignore the needs, but I would tell myself, "Oh, what this person is feeling or thinking about matters more than what I have going on because my thing is not as big or dramatic or severe." Throughout my life, I've had to learn that needs are needs. People get to express, share, and own their needs without those needs being measured. I think I can deny the importance of my needs. That's been the continual work when it comes to feeling needy.

—Faye

Another way Twos avoid their needs is by subconsciously expecting others to notice and meet their needs without the Two ever having to ask for help. Twos have a subconscious scorecard or tally sheet in the back of their minds, which they use to keep tabs on how much they've shown up for other people. The Two isn't usually aware of this scorekeeping until their needs aren't met by someone they have been generous and helpful with. When this happens, the scorecard becomes conscious, and the Two can feel angry and resentful, listing off all the times they've shown up for that person in the past. Because the superpower of this type is anticipating other people's needs before the person is even aware of those needs, Twos hold a subconscious expectation that others will do that for them too. *"If I can see that you're sad and I show up with flowers and food and hugs without you even having to ask, then when I am in need I expect you to show up for me, too, without me having to ask."* As a result, resentment can often arise when Twos feel like others do not appreciate their efforts or show up for them when the tables are turned.

For all of us, it can be a vulnerable thing to ask for help, to let people into the messy parts of our interior experiences, to admit that we don't actually have it all under control. To protect against this particular vulnerability, Twos simply don't ask for help and might even actively refuse or downplay their need for help when it is offered.

Since this type is in the Heart Center—or the image-management center—of the Enneagram, the emphasis here isn't on not having needs as much as it is on not being *seen* as needy. Remember that the primary objective of Heart types is to create an image that helps them be seen in a positive light for who they are and what they do. At the root of this avoidance of being seen as needy is the core fear of **rejection**. Twos believe that if they are perceived as needy by the important others in their lives, they will be rejected. Since the story of the Two states that people love them and accept them *because* of how good they are at meeting needs, Twos have a deep fear that if they are no longer useful in your life, you will move on and find someone else who can meet your needs better. It is hard and necessary work for a Two to practice remembering what is true: that even if they were unable to lift a finger in the service of anyone else, they would still be deserving of love.

At the core, I want to be loved, and I want to be seen, and I want to feel like I can show up fully. When I've been in places and spaces in the world where I haven't felt seen fully, that has felt like rejection. It feels like there are pieces of who I am or how I feel that I have to hide, or that you're just not seeing or hearing. When we think about this in the context of being Black, there are a lot of places and spaces in the world where it can really feel like a challenge to show up fully. What I've learned—and this is the tough work—is to name it for what it is. From the healthiest place and in the relationships with the people that I trust the most, I'm able to name it and say, "Hey, this thing happened, and I didn't feel seen." Those are the richest relationships because they can move the sense of tension in the body into a sense of expansion and lightness.

Rejection shows up as a threat to vulnerability. It says: don't practice it here; don't share that part here. I don't walk through the world seeing the threat of rejection everywhere. But there have been really critical or pivotal moments where I'm like, "Oh, this is what this feels like. And it really doesn't feel good." In those times when I really felt rejection and didn't know how to communicate it, I carried it in my body. It showed up as tension or sadness or a sense of grief that you carry with you. I found that the best way to navigate through it is with honesty and vulnerability and being real about it. I have this desire to be loved. I want you to see me. And so rejection really feels like not being seen and further than that, not being loved. And *that* is tough.

—Faye

DEFENSE MECHANISM

Repression

The defense mechanism that keeps this type structure going is called repression, which refers to the pattern of subduing personal needs in order to avoid being seen as needy and preserve the image of helpfulness. Twos find that they are often subconsciously repressing what *they* really need in order to attend to the needs of others who are important to them. This defense mechanism is different from simply denying your needs because, as mentioned earlier, Twos are aware of their needs for support, encouragement, care, and love. They just are afraid to allow themselves to own those needs and receive the love that is available to them. They believe they must be the river to still be needed.

One of my teachers who identifies as a Two has a practice of checking in with her own needs when she begins to experience the world around her as needy. As we saw in the avoidance section, Twos' repression of their own needs might be displaced on the external world as a way to give those needs validity. So, when Twos starts to think to themselves, *"Wow everyone is really needy right now and asking for so much,"* it might be an invitation to instead ask: *"Do I have a need I'm ignoring right now?"* This allows a Two to bring their attention in from the outside filled with others' needs into their own experience.

The pattern of repression gives rise to **pride**, which is the emotional habit of Twos. Pride for this type structure shows up in two different ways. First, there is the prideful inflation of self. Twos tend to believe they know best how to show up for others. Their aim is to make themselves indispensable in the lives of those important to them, and they can really begin to see themselves that way. This kind of pride says, *"I know what you need better than you do."* Or, *"You need me to survive."* The other side of pride is a deflation of self, a false humility. This pride says, *"Oh, I don't need anything, how can I help you?"* This is a tricky form of pride because it can appear on the surface like the Two really just wants to focus their energy on helping others, when in reality this pride habitually places the Two above everyone else in the role of giver.

This is why when Twos reconnect with Holy Freedom, when they remember that it is not their job to be the river for everyone else, they exude a sense of humility that acknowledges they have needs just like everyone else. Humility offers the freedom to see yourself as human, which offers the freedom to both receive and give.

For me, when I feel like my role on this earth is only to serve or help other people, then I've missed it. Because I think that often in that place, that's where depletion or being at capacity can show up. It's not wrong to help and serve; I love to do those things. They're really central to who I am. But I found a lot of freedom and a better way of helping people in centering love for myself. To say to myself, "Wow, I really care about you. I care about the needs that you have and the things that you feel. How do I honor that?" When I don't feel the pressure to be helpful all the time, it's because I've made a conscious effort to honor how I really feel, to nurture myself so I really feel a sense of freedom versus the sense of obligation. I find that I help, serve, and love people best when I really do it from this place of capacity and fullness and abundance. My capacity to love myself fully and show up for myself fully has expanded my capacity to love other people well. There's freedom, joy, and abundance in that. That's the place I like to live from, and I can almost feel the difference in my body. There's lightness, joy, happiness.

I think helpfulness for the Two is both the strength and the challenge. It's like this really cool asset or gift that you have. I think when it becomes armor is when the motivation isn't connected and the honesty isn't there. Helpfulness as armor can look like feeling like I'm the only person who can do this or I have to show up this way or if I don't help you, what does that mean for me? Will you reject me? So when the motivation becomes helping out of obligation or fear, it can feel like armor. I'm not always good at this. I think it's gonna be the lifelong work of being able to distinguish the two. But there are things, like paying attention to my body, that help me know the difference. I know the difference in my body between feeling freedom, lightness, joy, instead of feeling tension and frustration and burden.

—Faye

CREATING SPACE BETWEEN SELF AND ARMOR

Notice—Pause—Allow

Remember that your practice is to notice, pause, and allow what comes up to be there without judgment or shame. Let compassion, gratitude, and curiosity guide you as you use the following prompts and exercises to practice bringing awareness to your experience of the type structure. Below are some helpful ways to begin noticing the patterns of your type. The stress and security movements and somatic profile can help you begin to practice curiosity when you notice yourself showing up in these ways.

Stress and Security Movements

When Twos are experiencing stress, they move toward Eight. A conscious movement to Eight can offer Twos access to the Eight's assertive energy that can help Twos ask directly for what they need and create healthy boundaries for themselves in relationships. The unconscious movement to Eight can be challenging as Twos might explode with anger after enduring the consequences of their poor boundaries. They might begin to see everyone else as needy and demanding and grow resentful and angry.

When Twos are relaxed and feel secure, they move toward the space of the Four. A conscious movement to Four offers an invitation for Twos to become comfortable in their interior world. Here, Twos can explore what they want, how they actually feel, and who they are outside of others' needs. The challenge with an unconscious movement toward Four is that Twos can get stuck in sadness or melancholy if their attention is drawn only to what is missing in their relationships or themselves.

Somatic Profile

Twos hold a lot of their energy in their chests, diaphragms, and shoulders. Their upper bodies are expressive and energetic, but they tend to be disconnected from their lower bodies. One of my teachers refers to her experience of this as being a floating heart with no legs. Without connection to the ground, Twos tend to discharge their emotions and their anxiety through talking and relating with others.

Journal Prompts

Below are some prompts to help you begin to practice curiosity around the story of your type. Find a quiet place to reflect on these questions. Remember to be present with your body as you answer these prompts. Notice, pause, and allow. Be compassionate, curious, and grateful to your body for its intelligence. You can come back to this practice as often as you need to.

1. What is your earliest memory of feeling joyful and free? Where were you? Who were you with? What

were you doing? Pause to check in: How does your body feel right now as you write about it?

2. What would change about the way you live if it were true that you don't need to earn value or love by taking care of others' needs? Pause to check in: How does your body feel right now as you write about it?

3. What if it's true that you can be seen as needy and still be deserving of acceptance and love?

4. If you didn't *have* to be helpful all the time, who would you be free to be?

5. When is your armor of helpfulness necessary in your everyday life? When is it *not* necessary?

6. What does safety feel like in your body? Who do you feel safe with, enough to set down the armor? How does your body feel when you're with that person? Are you feeling some of that safety right now? You can always return to this space within yourself no matter what is happening outside of you.

Visualizations

Find a quiet place where you can relax without worry of interruption. If you are able, sit comfortably upright, uncrossing your hands and placing both feet flat on the floor. If you aren't able to do so, adjust your body to a position that helps you feel comfortable and grounded. Read through the prompt below, then close your eyes and begin to visualize. When you have completed the visualization, slowly bring your attention back to your body and the surface you are resting on, listen to the sounds around you, and open your eyes.

1. Visualize yourself picking up helpfulness and putting it on like armor. What does your armor look like? How does your body feel when you are carrying the armor?
2. Visualize yourself taking off the armor of helpfulness and setting it down. How does your body feel when you imagine setting down the armor in a safe space?

Community Practice

Often, we subconsciously weaponize our armor against others. If we live by a singular story, we try to subject others to that singular story as well. Because you believe you must be seen as helpful to have value and be loved, you might dismiss others who don't need you or manufacture needs for them that you can fulfill. Because you avoid your own neediness, you might manipulate others into meeting your needs. As you create space between yourself and your armor, I encourage you to consider how you require those around you to fit into your singular story. As you become more comfortable being with your own needs, you will increase your capacity to stay grounded in the face of other people's needs.

Chapter 12

TYPE FOUR: EXCEPTIONALITY AS ARMOR

NICKNAMES	The Romantic, The Individualist
ARMOR	Exceptionality
HOLY IDEA	Origin
VIRTUE/ESSENCE QUALITY	Equanimity
MENTAL HABIT	Melancholy
EMOTIONAL HABIT	Longing

HOLY IDEA

HOLY ORIGIN: The Aspen Grove

Imagine you are a tall tree—let's say an aspen tree—on a hillside. You are one of thousands, and you resemble your other grove members with whitish bark and little oval leaves that flutter and dance in the slightest wind. Above ground, it might seem as though there are many individual trees all clustered together on this hillside. But you're aware of what isn't readily obvious on the surface–that this entire grove of thousands of trees is actually just one singular living organism. Deep down in your roots, you feel and sense the connection to every other aspen tree in that forest. You all derive from the same origin–the first roots that kept replicating and keep you all connected underneath the soil. You are fed and sustained through this deep connection underneath the soil. Your growth into maturity is supported by this root system. And there is literally nothing you could do to extricate yourself from this connection. Even if you were cut down, the original root system–and your connection to it–cannot be fully extinguished.

In this grove, nothing of substance is missing. You are both a part of the whole and the whole itself. In this space of wholeness and connection, you receive the sunlight and nutrients you need to flourish. There is no competition here; because everyone is fed and nourished by their connection to the massive root system underneath, there is no need to fight for connection or earn it.

This is a depiction of **Holy Origin**, the objective reality, or Holy Idea, associated with the Type Four structure. Holy Origin is *the original state of being in which we experience whole and complete connection in every moment with nothing of importance missing or lacking.* Holy Origin invites us into remembering that we are connected to the source of life, and because that connection is secure, we have nothing to earn or prove in order to gain connection, acceptance, and love. It invites us into the rest and gratitude that is experienced when we are not constantly striving to prove that we are enough in order to be loved.

When Fours are disconnected from this objective reality, they begin to see themselves as separate from the connection that others experience. They see themselves as solo trees, cut off from the sustenance of the root system, and believe that something about who they are disqualifies them from connection. They might organize their lives around becoming whatever they believe makes them deserving of being accepted into the grove again. Real experiences of pain and loss might be elevated as proof that they don't deserve to belong, and they might become overidentified with the story of being an outsider.

However, when they remember and reconnect with the truth of Holy Origin, they exude the virtue of **equanimity**, which simply means a state of balance and harmony with what exists. Equanimity allows the Four to be present with what is true, for example, that painful things can happen to you without being a reflection of your deficiency or deserved lack of belonging.

IDEALIZATION

Exceptional, Unique, Authentic

When Fours experience pain in their formative years, the story that forms as a way to keep them safe is, "*I must be seen as unique or exceptional to be loved.*" Fours believe they have to offer something original and different from others in order to be seen as worthy of love. If they feel disconnected from the grove of trees—their true home—they believe that the best way to get an invitation to return home is by standing out. Standing out gets the attention of the other trees who might then notice the left-out Fours and invite them back into the circle of connection. Sometimes the push for Black excellence—the need to always show up and stand out as incredible and spectacular—can have this Type Four flavor to it, especially when the excellence is wielded as proof of worthiness. The reality is that who we are on a boring, regular day is already deserving of love, but the story of the Four asserts that it is only the exceptional and unique parts of us that are deserving of acceptance and love.

For the Four, being seen as unique can easily become transactional. *"I offer you this different, interesting, and unique take on life, art, spirituality, or anything else; you see my value and give me acceptance and love in return."* Often Fours will push back on this idealization, stating that they don't make a concerted effort to be seen as unique. This is partly true because, as we've explored already, the idealization takes something that is already true about the type and turns it into a singular story. Fours are naturally gifted at seeing the uniqueness in things without effort. Fours are good at finding viewpoints, angles, and narratives that are often overlooked by other people and making those different viewpoints compelling and beautiful.

Fours tend to be naturally creative, empathic, highly sensitive people. They are unafraid of taking deep and long dives into spaces others would steer clear of. Spaces like grief, loss, and even death are not scary to Fours, whose high emotional intelligence and capacity for depth make them excellent listeners and escorts for those journeying through dark places. They are constantly doing these deep dives into the dark places of their own stories and feel more comfortable swimming in the depths than skimming the surface. Fours invite us to see beauty in places we wouldn't naturally expect—in the dark and painful places, in the outsiders and the overlooked. Since Fours see themselves often as outsiders, this invitation is also for others to see *them* as beautiful and worth noticing. Fours want to feel special so that they are not easily overlooked and forgotten. The flip side of the constant need to be seen as unique is the loneliness that comes from being perceived as different all the time. Fours think their uniqueness is what will earn them connection, and instead they discover that this need to be different can keep them feeling separate from the connection that is already available.

Internally I strive to be exceptional in a lot of my own ways, related to my childhood experiences and what I noticed would make me feel good enough for my parents. I'm trying to undo a lot of that. I've been able to make a shift from being exceptional or reaching this certain bar that I've set for myself, and I actually just try to be good enough. That's been my mantra recently. I want to feel like what I did at the end of the day is good enough. Instead of trying to meet the ideal of what I think is exceptional, or what I've been conditioned to feel like is exceptional, in how I show up emotionally, I ask myself: "Was what I was able to give today good enough? And was I being true to me?" Otherwise, I often feel like I didn't do enough or I wasn't enough.

—Chanel

Fours believe they have to be authentic, or true to who they really are, in order to be loved. And yet, Fours still make their home in this image-driven, shape-shifting Heart Center of the Enneagram. This desire to be seen in a positive light while also wanting to remain true to themselves creates a false authenticity in Fours—an image of authenticity that they believe will earn them love. If, for example, a Four believes that being seen as wise, serious, and introspective is what earns them acceptance and love, the type structure will work hard to make sure that image is what projects at all times, *whether or not it is reflective of what is true in that moment*. If they find themselves feeling lighthearted, wanting to crack jokes or stay on the surface of conversations, the type structure will push down what is their true authenticity in that moment in favor of the preferred *image* of authenticity. True authenticity requires allowing yourself to be present with what is occurring in the moment rather than trying to shape the moment to fit the image you desire.

There is an unfortunate stereotype about Fours that gets thrown around often. Fours are often described as liking suffering or pain. I haven't yet met or worked with a Four who admits to enjoying pain or suffering. Now, Fours *do* have an incredible capacity to withstand suffering and even tend to overidentify with suffering. To understand why this is the case, let's play with a metaphor. Imagine you are a child again and you experience something painful and out of the ordinary. Let's say this painful experience materializes as a baby elephant in the middle of the room. As children do, you look to the adults around you to help soothe you and make sense of the pain you're experiencing. Let's imagine that the adults completely ignore the baby elephant, and rather than soothe you, they tell you to stop focusing so much on the negatives. Maybe they tell you to suck it up and stop being so sensitive or to look on the bright side, or they might even question your pain, saying, *"What elephant are you talking about? I don't see any elephants in here."* But you can see the elephant in the middle of the room, even though everyone walks around it like it isn't there. You learn to distrust their happiness because it seems like pretense—the people telling you to choose happiness are not addressing the elephant of pain in the room.

You start to wonder if making it bigger will finally get them to acknowledge the elephant. You befriend the elephant, tend to the elephant, make it your mission to make sure that no one forgets that it's there. The elephant keeps getting bigger, and you keep checking in with the adults around you: *"Do you see it yet? Can we talk about it yet? Is my pain valid enough to be acknowledged yet?"* If they still don't acknowledge the elephant, you carry it on your back with you everywhere you go, waiting and hoping for someone outside of you to validate that they see it too–that you're not crazy and your pain is real. That is, until you realize that your own gaze is enough. When you realize that you no longer have to wait for someone outside of you to validate your pain in order for it to be real, you begin to heal.

Fours are comfortable with sadness and suffering because they've carried their giant elephants of pain around with them for so long. It isn't enjoyable, but it is a familiar heaviness, almost like the comforting weight of a heavy blanket. This is why the mental habit of Type Four is **melancholy**, a natural affinity toward sadness. It must be hard not to feel the weight of sadness when the elephant of pain lives on your back all of the time. While an over-emphasis on optimism or positivity can feel offensive to Fours, the work of healing invites them into expansive joy instead, in which there is room to hold both grief and hope, light and dark, pain and joy, without dismissing one for the other.

AVOIDANCE

Ordinariness, Inadequacy, Deficiency

If you must be seen as an original, someone unique and exceptional, in order to be loved, then being seen as ordinary is what the type structure works to avoid at all costs. Fours would much prefer the high-highs and the low-lows over the boring middle. Experiencing the highs, Fours can begin to see themselves as superior to others. Their sense of importance is based on being more interesting than or more unique than or more original than the next person. Others who aren't interesting enough for the Four are avoided as well. What is true here for the Four is true for us all—often what we dislike and avoid in other people reveals what we dislike and avoid in ourselves.

While experiencing the lows, Fours see themselves as inferior to the idealized version of themselves or other people they see as ideal. Everyone else somehow got the manual or the cheat sheet to pass the test of acceptance, and Fours feel like they were skipped over. They see themselves as permanently on the outside of connection, never enough or too much. In this space, Fours retreat into themselves and can be prone to bouts of depression.

Fours have an internal ongoing story that tells them that, at their core, they are deficient. As we saw at the beginning of the chapter, when Fours are connected to Holy Origin, they know that nothing of substance is missing. When the type structure is in the driver's seat, however, Fours become preoccupied with what's missing from their experiences. Most frequently, they are preoccupied with what's missing within themselves. The story of deficiency tells Fours that they are inherently lacking a key ingredient that would make them deserving of love without effort. They believe everyone else has it but them. Of course, this feeling of permanent deficiency is painful, which is why the type structure seeks to avoid it by creating an image of being spectacular and special to compensate for the internal feelings of lack.

THE ENNEAGRAM FOR BLACK LIBERATION

I have a really bad habit of feeling like I'm a pioneer for a lot of things that are uncool, and then the minute they become cool or catch on, I don't want to be a part of it anymore. It feels like a never-ending journey of finding something that feels true to me, something that I really like and brings me joy but that other people aren't doing, so that I can have a sense of uniqueness.

That's one way, on a superficial level, that I avoid feeling ordinary and try to be unique. Sometimes, it comes out in how I show up for others. I want to make others feel held and special and understood in ways that I would want myself. I feel like that helps me hold on to my uniqueness while showing up for others too.

—Chanel

If the image does its job, then the Four can earn love without anyone having to know that on the inside they are not as shiny as the image they've created. This is why one of the characteristics of this type structure is a push-pull dynamic in relationships. Fours crave intimacy and are simultaneously terrified of it. They want you to really see them and know them, but greater than the desire for intimacy is the fear that if you get too close, you will see beneath the shiny image and confirm their inner sense of deficiency and lack. So when you get too close, they push you away, even though what they crave is that kind of intimacy.

The core fear underneath this pattern of avoidance is **abandonment**. Fours avoid being seen as ordinary and inadequate because they are deeply terrified that if you see their deficiencies you will leave. As is true for all of the Heart types, they believe that who they are at their core isn't enough and that they must do something to earn love and connection. The catch for Fours is that they abandon themselves when they go outside of themselves to create an image to earn love.

Thinking about the fear of abandonment makes me super emotional. Growing up, there was a time when my mom and I were abandoned. I think I have always felt like I could have prevented it, even though I was a kid. So as an adult, it kind of shows up as a strong sense of "I didn't deserve that." I didn't deserve that abandonment. It's something that I'll beat myself up over. I know that I didn't deserve the abandonment, but then I try to figure out ways to avoid it happening again. I try to set up a barrier to abandonment by planning for it. If I plan for that abandonment, if I set it up in my head and know this is how it's gonna feel, then I'll be emotionally prepared. I tell myself: "You're going to feel betrayed, you're going to feel hurt, you're going to feel like it's your fault. So, let's plan for it so that when it happens, you're prepared." And it may never happen, so I could be putting my energy into preparing for something that may not happen.

—Chanel

DEFENSE MECHANISM

Introjection

Fours wait for an external invitation to their own worthiness, value, and lovability. As a type found in the Heart Center, much of their own sense of value comes from the external world. If the external world sees a Four as valuable, then they must be. The opposite is true: if Fours feel as though the external world sees them as lacking in value, that also must be true of them. We see this pattern of handing over one's own value to others in all three of the Heart types. Across this center, the belief is this: *"How you see me is how I must be."* This is why image management is so important to Heart types—because of this idea that how you are seen determines how much love and acceptance you have access to.

We call this pattern introjection in the Four type structure, and it refers to the unconscious adoption of others' ideas and attitudes. Introjection can be positive or negative. Positive introjection can look like taking in others' positive ideas of who you are as true to you. If enough people say you are creative and inspiring, then you must be. Negative introjection looks like the opposite, taking in others' negative ideas of who you are as true. If others say you are mean and spiteful, then you must be. Whether positive or negative, introjection works by accepting external information about your value without a filter grounded in truth.

Fours often feel like their sense of self is shaky, like they are unsure of who they really are. This is why the opinions of others are so important to them because those opinions help them construct a sense of self, regardless of how true or untrue it is.

Fours spend a lot of time in the emotional habit of **longing** for what is missing. They are almost always longing for what is missing within themselves (a sturdy sense of self grounded in truth) and what's missing in their relationships or life pursuits. They believe there is something or someone out there that can help them regain this lost sense of connection to who they really are and the acceptance they crave, and they find themselves longing for that constantly. What they fail to see is that they are the ones they are longing for.

The antidote to the fear of abandonment is the practice of coming home to oneself. When you belong to yourself, that belonging isn't up for debate and can never be taken away. This allows a Four to grieve the very real pain of loss without becoming the lost thing. The work for a Four is to begin to build a filter, one that is grounded in the truth of who they really are. No one outside of us can give us value. That value is inherent, and when a Four is connected to that reality, they are better able to experience other people's praise or disappointment without letting it determine their value or worth.

If I didn't have to be exceptional all the time, I wouldn't feel shame in embracing all the facets of myself. I would be able to accept the emotions that arise without feeling ashamed when other people see those sides of me. I would be able to trust other people with my pain and not just suffer in silence. I would give myself the space to be vulnerable in front of other people in ways that don't feel like I'm emotionally exploding. People's expectations of how I should show up affect me. To a lot of people, I'm always very happy or "sunny." A huge amount of the time, that is true, but it can also sometimes shoot you in the foot when that is how other people expect you to always show up. When you're not that way, they drastically notice and ask if you're upset. That "sunny" part of me is a huge part of my identity, but there are other parts of me that are just as equally okay and acceptable and good. My hair's always been a huge outlet for my creativity, so people expect me to change my hair often. When I don't, they're like, "Oh, my God, what's happening?" And people expect me to always have different clothes and stand out in that sense, like I'm always this bag of self-expression. I feel like I'm always expected to be sunny and creative, and it makes it hard to be vulnerable.

I feel like my armor of exceptionality is necessary when I don't have trust. Trust is huge for me—being able to feel like I can trust someone emotionally, trust someone to make me feel safe, to be able to be my whole self and be able to share my fears, my joys, and all of that stuff. I feel like when trust is truly there, I don't need that shield. But if I don't have trust, and I'm still really getting to know people, I'm very careful. I'm an open book if you ask me a question or if you want to know more about me; I will share probably anything. But I won't give up that information without people first asking me to. Even with people that I fully trust, there's always still some hesitancy in the back of my mind. I find myself wondering, "Can I really truly trust you to hold all of this?" Even if people have proven themselves, I still always have that fear in the back of my mind, but for the most part I can crack open quite a bit and not have a shield if there is a lot of trust there.

—Chanel

CREATING SPACE BETWEEN SELF AND ARMOR

Notice—Pause—Allow

Remember that your practice is to notice, pause, and allow what comes up to be there without judgment or shame. Let compassion, gratitude, and curiosity guide you as you use the following prompts and exercises to practice bringing awareness to your experience of the type structure. Below are some helpful ways to begin noticing the patterns of your type. The stress and security movements and somatic profile can help you begin to practice curiosity when you notice yourself showing up in these ways.

Stress and Security Movements

When Fours are experiencing stress, they move toward Two. A conscious movement to Two can bring Fours out of their interior world where they often get lost and feel isolated or lonely. In the Two space, Fours are able to bring into focus the experiences and needs of people outside of themselves. The unconscious movement to Two can be challenging as Fours might feel like they are losing their individuality in focusing so much on others. They might find it stressful to balance their need for individuality with the relational demands of others.

When Fours are relaxed and feel secure, they move toward the space of the One. A conscious movement to One offers access to the Body Center's sense of groundedness and calm. In this space, Fours have the capacity to experience their emotions without getting stuck in them. They are more consistent, practical, and move forward into action that helps right what is wrong rather than simply focus on what is missing. The challenge with an unconscious movement toward One is that Fours might become too critical of others in their effort to improve the world around them.

Somatic Profile

Fours' energy is collected toward the middle of the body, particularly the chest area. There tends to be less energy in the hands and feet, as Fours spend a lot of time exploring their feelings. Especially because Fours tend to favor the melancholic feelings like sadness or grief, the weightiness of these emotions can result in anxiety or hyperventilation.

Expressive activities that utilize the periphery of the body (hands and feet) can be helpful to help Fours create balance in their bodies.

Journal Prompts

Below are some prompts to help you begin to practice curiosity around the story of your type. Find a quiet place to reflect on these questions. Remember to be present with your body as you answer these prompts. Notice, pause, and allow. Be compassionate, curious, and grateful to your body for its intelligence. You can come back to this practice as often as you need to.

1. What is your earliest memory of feeling joyful and free? Where were you? Who were you with? What were you doing? Pause to check in: How does your body feel right now as you write about it?

2. What would change about the way you live if it were true that you don't need to earn value or love by offering something unique or exceptional to others? Pause to check in: How does your body feel right now as you write about it?

3. What if it's true that you can be seen as ordinary, even inadequate, and still be deserving of acceptance and love?

4. If you didn't *have* to be exceptional all the time, who would you be free to be?

5. When is your armor of exceptionality necessary in your everyday life? When is it *not* necessary?

6. What does safety feel like in your body? Who do you feel safe with, enough to set down the armor? How does your body feel when you're with that person? Are you feeling some of that safety right now? You can always return to this space within yourself no matter what is happening outside of you.

Visualizations

Find a quiet place where you can relax without worry of interruption. If you are able, sit comfortably upright, uncrossing your hands and placing both feet flat on the floor. If you aren't able to do so, adjust your body to a position that helps you feel comfortable and grounded. Read through the prompt below, then close your eyes and begin to visualize. When you have completed the visualization, slowly bring your attention back to your body and the surface you are resting on, listen to the sounds around you, and open your eyes.

1. Visualize yourself picking up exceptionality and putting it on like armor. What does your armor look like? How does your body feel when you are carrying the armor?
2. Visualize yourself taking off the armor of exceptionality and setting it down. How does your body feel when you imagine setting down the armor in a safe space?

Community Practice

Often, we subconsciously weaponize our armor against others. If we live by a singular story, we try to subject others to that singular story as well. Because you believe you must be seen as unique or exceptional to be accepted and loved, you might dismiss others who don't see you the way you want to be seen. Because you avoid being seen as ordinary, you might avoid, and feel superior to, others whom you see as uninteresting or boring. As you create space between yourself and your armor, I encourage you to consider how you require those around you to fit into your singular story. As you become more comfortable being with your ordinariness, you will increase your capacity to make space for others' ordinariness too.

Chapter 13

THE HEAD CENTER

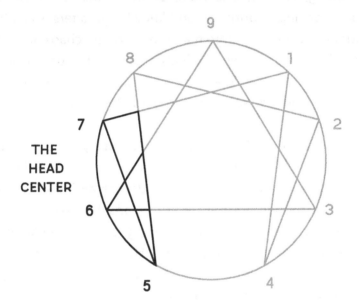

The Head Center is the seat of our mental intelligence, which gives us the ability to conceptualize, analyze, and synthesize information. With this center, we try to understand the differences and similarities between things, focusing on both the big picture and how all the little elements fit into the bigger picture.

Head types are always acutely aware of the "data" that exists in the environment, noticing everything and sorting

THE ENNEAGRAM FOR BLACK LIBERATION

the data in order to make sense of the world around them. For this triad, life is a mystery to be solved, and solving it requires paying attention to the information and sorting it in a way that offers meaning and clarifies the bigger picture. Life can be experienced as confusing, illogical, overwhelming, chaotic, uncertain, or even unsafe for Head types. Seeking information and knowledge offers a way to understand and therefore make sense of the chaos around them. They seek answers to life's questions through observation and analysis. These types focus on the search for meaning and certainty by studying things and figuring them out.

The core needs for this triad are for **safety**, security, certainty, possibilities, predictability, and assurance. The head is used as a means to get these needs met, and when those needs are threatened, the core emotions that arise are fear and anxiety. Head types have a strong fear of the unknown or of not knowing enough. For a Head type, knowledge is safety, or at the very least, the acquisition of knowledge defends against the discomfort of confusion and uncertainty. A friend of mine who identifies as a Five said to me, "Life is illogical, so I use my head to make it logical."

Head types also fear not being prepared to meet and manage the chaos of the world. This triad believes that if you have all the information you need, you can be prepared and avoid feeling helpless, overwhelmed, or trapped in distressing situations. And yet, we all still have to contend with the chaos, uncertainty, and pain of life despite our best attempts to escape. Fives, Sixes, and Sevens move even further into their heads to escape experiencing the present reality of their pain.

In this triad, the head is used to avoid being fully present in the body, which is the only part of us that is always in the present moment. Whether escaping into gathering knowledge, fun and pleasure, or prepping for danger, the mind is used to create an upward displacement of what's really happening in the heart and body. As we will explore with types Six and Seven in particular, much of the collective coping mechanisms of Black culture in the United States utilize the core themes of the Head Center to keep from being overwhelmed by fear or pain.

Fives manage their fear by gathering as much information as they can about things they find interesting and useful, storing their knowledge away to give themselves a sense of self-sufficiency and safety. Sixes manage their fear by threat forecasting—analyzing every possible worst-case scenario that could occur and making plans to keep themselves and their loved ones safe should any of those scenarios occur. Sevens manage their fear by ignoring the worst-case scenarios or difficulties and hyperfocusing on planning for possibilities and opportunities that can keep them insulated from pain.

When this triad is able to come home to who they truly are and reconnect with their inherent capacity to face life's uncertainties, they find the courage to lean more into trust— trusting life and others enough to risk being fully present. Living, for them, becomes more of an embodied practice rather than an intellectual exercise.

Chapter 14

TYPE SIX: VIGILANCE AS ARMOR

NICKNAMES	The Loyal Skeptic, The Loyalist
ARMOR	Vigilance
HOLY IDEA	Faith
VIRTUE/ESSENCE QUALITY	Courage
MENTAL HABIT	Doubt
EMOTIONAL HABIT	Fear

HOLY IDEA

HOLY FAITH: The Walk in the Woods

Picture yourself on a long, leisurely walk through the woods on a beautiful day. The sun is shining bright, but a cool breeze keeps the temperature pleasant. You notice the crawling insects, the call of the flying birds, the insects that buzz by, the rustle of the leaves in the wind. You feel at peace and at one with your environment. The trail you're on begins to curve, and you wonder what you might find on the other side of the bend. When you've rounded the corner, you see a beautiful vista in the distance, but a fallen branch from a nearby tree blocks the path. You walk up to it, climb over it, and continue on your way.

As you continue to explore, you sense that you are no longer alone in this part of the woods. You listen to and observe your immediate environment. Even though you don't see any animals around you, your intuition tells you to pause right where you are. You do so, and a moment later, you watch as an elk and its calf appear and walk across the path to the other side of the woods. You are in awe of the enormous beast, but you don't sense that you are in danger. Once the elk has disappeared from sight, you continue on your journey to the beautiful vista ahead.

This is a depiction of **Holy Faith**, the objective reality, or Holy Idea, associated with the Type Six structure. Holy Faith is *a true faith in self, others, and the universe*, encompassing the knowing that our core is made of up essence and our essence is indestructible. This knowing, also called Holy Strength, allows us to enter each moment with confidence and a trust that we will not be destroyed. Holy Faith also offers access to a more grounded perception of reality that allows us to see others as full of possibility for connection rather than potential threats.

When Sixes are disconnected from Holy Faith, the pleasant woods quickly transform into a dangerous, threatening jungle that becomes a survival-of-the-fittest nightmare. Sixes believe there is danger lurking around every corner, everyone is a potential threat, and that they will not have what it takes to protect themselves from being destroyed. To prevent this, they spend all their energy scanning for danger. They might miss out on the pleasant sights and sounds of the woods in their hyperfocus on danger and threats. They lose contact with their intuition, which is what offered helpful guidance in the imagery above. Instead, they become more attuned to their heightened signals of fear and anxiety, finding it difficult to differentiate between the voices of their intuition and their fear. They might leave the scary woods altogether, if they can, or they might try to overcompensate for their fear by purposefully seeking out the dangers in the woods.

When a Six reconnects to Holy Faith, they exude the virtue of **courage**. For a Six whose habit of scanning for threats might keep them from taking action, courage allows them to move forward purposely even while acknowledging their fear. It reminds them that multiple things can be true at once—they can be afraid and they can still move forward at the same time. With courage, a Six is able to learn how to be present with their fear and soothe it so that they have greater access to their intuition.

IDEALIZATION

Vigilant, Cautiously Loyal

When Sixes are disconnected from the objective reality of Holy Faith, they create a subjective story that says that the only way to ensure safety and security in a dangerous world is to be vigilant about everything and to find something or someone outside of themselves to be loyal to in exchange for safety. Sixes become skeptical and vigilant, untrusting of everything and everyone until they can prove safety. To them, the world is unpredictable and unsafe, and the best way to protect yourself is to always remain on guard. This pattern of behavior leads to the mental habit of **doubt** in Sixes. Sixes doubt both their own perceptions and others' motives and might test and question others until they can prove they are safe.

Sixes are naturally loyal, trustworthy, thoughtful, and dependable people. They are incredible friends to have. They show up with an inviting warmth and protectiveness over their own. Sixes are also naturally intuitive people, but when the type structure is in the driver's seat, that intuition is lost beneath the type's overarching tendency toward fear and anxiety. Sixes see the world as an unpredictable place, but disconnected from their intuition, they are unsure how to best ensure security. Instead, they look outward to find belief systems or authority figures to keep them safe. This external authority lays out for the Six what is safe and what isn't, what to lean into and what to avoid. This external authority could be a religious belief system, and it is said that the most common Enneagram type in religious circles is the Six. Religion offers a clear delineation between what to do and what to avoid, and this sort of clarity allows a Six to create some predictability.

Playing by the rules is also very important to Sixes. Safety is seen as the absence of uncertainty and unpredictability.

Rules outline a certain and predictable expectation for behavior, which helps Sixes feel safe and supported. In fact, one of the stressors for a Six is other people not playing by the rules. This isn't necessarily about right and wrong as we see in the Type One structure; it is more about anxiety and safety. For example, if we all followed the rules and slowed down when the green light changed to yellow, the Six wouldn't have to feel anxious about the rogue rule breakers who speed through yellow lights and potentially endanger others. Rule following for Sixes is about eliminating the uncertainty and unpredictability that makes them feel unsafe.

When I think of being cautious, what comes to mind is hypersensitivity. Gauging the temperature of the room, gauging other people's interactions with one other, with me. It's this constant measuring, testing. I feel like I'm constantly testing little bits of information or leaving bits of myself out there and watching to see how those bits are received. If they're not received well, I tuck them back in my pouch. I think that's a lot of where my energy lies—assessing whether or not this is a safe place for me to be. And by safe, I mean: Can I bring all of myself here? A lot of times, the answer is no, to be honest. When I was younger, I used to call myself a chameleon. I can assess what is valued in a space and bring that and be okay, survive, and even thrive. It was never about bringing my whole self, it was always about bringing the parts

THE ENNEAGRAM FOR BLACK LIBERATION

of me that were acceptable. I think I'm very skilled at it. I'm good at it. It's how I've survived. I think part of being cautious and vigilant was in a lot of ways a form of survival, not a path to thriving or being whole.

—Ruthie Mengistu Williams

Sixes develop two very distinct stances to gain security and safety. The *phobic* stance is an accommodating stance. A phobic Six tends to obey authority and avoid the threatening, scary things by staying where it is safe. This stance is characterized by fear. These Sixes are highly aware of their fears and take action to avoid the possibility of the fears coming true. The other stance is the *counterphobic* stance, which is more challenging in nature. Counterphobic Sixes defy authority and seek to fight and overcome perceived threats. This stance is characterized by aggression, and counterphobic Sixes often might look like Type Eights in their aggression. These Sixes tend to deny their fears by overcompensating. To give an oversimplified example, if a phobic Six is scared of heights, they will probably avoid skydiving and hiking to the peaks of mountains. If a counterphobic Six is scared of heights, they will most likely sign up for skydiving to prove that they can meet and beat their fear of heights. Sixes can exhibit both phobic and counterphobic stances in different areas of their lives, but usually, one stance is most common for each Six.

It is important to note that meeting fear with aggression isn't the same thing as courage. The aggression of a counterphobic Six is still fueled by fear. Fear is still in the driver's seat deciding what is a threat and compelling the Six to fight. This type of Six wants to eliminate fear and all the things that bring up uncertainty in their life, so they take a warlike approach to seek out and eliminate fear all the while denying they feel any. Courage, on the other hand, invites us to accept the fear *and* still move forward with firmness of purpose. When we are being courageous, we neither run from fear nor deny its presence. Courage allows us to be honest with ourselves and our own experiences.

AVOIDANCE

Uncertainty, Rejection

Since Sixes believe that they must be vigilant and cautiously loyal in order to gain security and safety, the type structure works hard to avoid uncertainty and unpredictability. One of the ways Sixes avoid uncertainty is by seeking multiple opinions in their decision-making. Especially in the phobic stance, Sixes lack confidence in their ability to make good decisions. These Sixes constantly second-guess themselves and will seek out second, third, and thirteenth opinions in order to make sure that the decision they are about to make is the safest one.

Phobic Sixes might also become unquestioningly loyal to authority figures, belief systems, or causes. Being a part of something or belonging to a group offers the kind of safety that standing on your own doesn't, and these Sixes will give their undying loyalty in order to feel safe and avoid uncertainty. They also tend to work hard to ensure that they aren't rejected by maintaining the trust and goodwill of others, caring for others within their group in a subconscious bid to assure their own safety. They try to avoid contradicting or opposing the people on whom they depend for their security.

> I avoid uncertainty through detachment. I call myself an escape artist. My main method is to avoid, so if there are difficult conversations or relationships, I just avoid those people. If there are difficult work projects, I will avoid them. Even if I'm alone by myself, it can feel like there are things coming at me, and so again I avoid. It can be through food or television, but even with television, you're not gonna catch me watching anything emotionally heavy. I am afraid it will awaken something in me, so I need a story or something to be lost in as a way to escape the uncertainty. I can't turn it off—it's always there, so I just turn my attention somewhere else.
>
> **—Ruthie Mengistu Williams**

Counterphobic Sixes tend to question everyone and everything. They are constantly looking for double messages and playing devil's advocate. They challenge and test authority figures to make sure those people are truly trustworthy before handing over their trust. They also test the other relationships in their lives, never quite trusting people fully. It is quite a process to gain a Six's trust, and once that trust is lost, it is almost impossible to gain it back.

Others might experience them as controlling, challenging, or pessimistic. While this may seem counterintuitive to the Six's goal of avoiding uncertainty and rejection, remember that the use of aggression in counterphobic Sixes is to identify and eliminate uncertainty. This testing behavior is their attempt to discover whether or not people are reliable before they give them their trust.

Sixes also use threat forecasting as a way to avoid uncertainty and rejection. Their minds are always ten steps ahead of the present moment, trying to identify and predict what could go wrong. If their bodies are approaching the corner of a street, their minds have already gone around the corner, anticipating the threatening possibilities they could face. Because of this habit of threat forecasting, they are always prepared in the event of danger. Since they see the world as unpredictable and threatening, they believe that predicting potential problems and worst-case scenarios will give them a plan and a sense of control when the danger does show up. While other types might be shocked in the face of danger, Sixes spring into action, unsurprised because they were predicting this all along.

Fueling this avoidant behavior is the core fear of **helplessness**. Sixes are terrified of ending up helpless or not in control in the face of danger. They don't want to be caught off guard by harmful situations and end up dependent on others for their safety. This fear keeps the armor of vigilance up, keeping Sixes in the story that says, "*I must be vigilant and loyal in order to be safe and secure in a threatening world.*"

Type Six is a common mistype for Black folks because of how necessary this particular armor is for our survival in this society. The hypervigilance, threat forecasting, and prepping for danger is a part of everyday life for many who hold marginalized identities. When I first came to the Enneagram, I mistyped myself as a Six because this armor felt so familiar to me, and it took me months to realize that the Six stance wasn't actually my primary home base but just an additional layer of armor I had to carry to survive in a truly threatening world.

> When I think of ending up helpless, I think of it as a failure. I failed at self-protection. I failed, and all that caution was for nothing. Physically, I feel a knot in the back of my neck. My jaw tightens up. I spend a lot of my energy assessing and identifying the danger zones so that I don't go where there's danger and instead stay where it's safe. So if I end up where there's danger, I have failed with the one thing that I was striving to do this whole time.
>
> —Ruthie Mengistu Williams

DEFENSE MECHANISM

Projection

Sixes use projection as a way to maintain the story of vigilance and avoid uncertainty and rejection. Projection is the unconscious process of transferring your own interior experience onto others. For Sixes who experience a heightened state of alarm internally, projection allows them to cast their own fears onto the world and people around them. Since the type structure is concerned with avoiding or eliminating fear, Sixes find it difficult to be present with and honest about their own heightened fear responses. Instead, they project their fears outward, and the world becomes a dangerous, threatening place. People become untrustworthy and out to get them or harm them in some way. Projection is sneaky, as all our defense mechanisms are, and so Sixes don't realize that they are the ones who have painted the world with this broad brushstroke of fear. Rather than saying, *"I am scared that if I am vulnerable, I will get hurt,"* projection teaches Sixes to say instead, *"People are mean and hurtful, and I have to protect myself from them."*

The difference between these two statements is ownership. It takes courage to name and own our fears, while cowardice leads us to deny or avoid fear. For Sixes whose emotional habit is **fear**, taking ownership over their own fears and anxiety is scary because they are disconnected from their foundational sense of self. Since they are afraid that they do not have what it takes to be okay internally, they project their internal world outward in order to have a sense of control. Sixes show a hyper-responsibility toward the people and environments around them but a lack of responsibility toward their internal worlds. To them, they experience fear and anxiety *only* because the world is a fearful, threatening place. The belief is that if fear and threats can be eliminated "out there," Sixes can feel safe within themselves.

I remember a Six telling a story about her experience with a new person who was added to her team at work. This Six explained that during their first meeting, she immediately felt as though this new member didn't really like her or even want to be a part of the team. She became increasingly convinced about this as she continued to interact with the team member for a few weeks. Then one day she realized that *she* was the one who didn't like the new team member and was upset that this person had been added to their team! She had come to feel a sense of safety within her team, and the addition of a new member disrupted that sense of safety. This was her own internal experience all along, but it was projected onto the unsuspecting new teammate. The Six's response to her teammate was really all about her own need for safety, and without building awareness of her type structure, projection would have kept her believing that this person was truly out to get her.

While it is absolutely true that the world can be threatening and unsafe—especially for those who are not protected by systems of power—that is a single-sided view of the multidimensional nature of our world. When Sixes are able to courageously own their fear, they can begin to learn how to soothe their bodies' experiences of fear, which can give them a greater capacity to experience what else is true about the world. Being able to say, "*I am scared that if I am vulnerable, I will get hurt*," allows more space for a Six to be open to the possibility that there are people who can hold their vulnerability with care and kindness.

If I didn't have to be cautious or vigilant all the time, I could allow myself to sing and dance. I'm aware of when I have been more free, and it is a more vibrant me. I think about wearing vibrant colors–bright blue and emerald and yellow. I think I wouldn't be so concerned with blending in, and I would allow myself to really be seen regardless of others' reception or verdict. Also, if I didn't have to be cautious all the time, I would be more joyful.

There are certain people that I've interacted with that have proven themselves to be untrustworthy, whether it is with information that I've given them or the way I've seen them handle other people's information. I think my armor of vigilance is necessary because they have not proven themselves to be safe places, for me or for anyone else. I think the armor is necessary when I have been hurt before by a person or situation. Fool me once, but you won't play me again!

Where my armor doesn't feel necessary is with the people that already have a track record of being safe places. My marriage is one relationship where all he has proven and shown me is, "I'm for you. I'm here; I'm not going anywhere." So when I start becoming armored with him, it doesn't compute for him. He'll remind me of the reality that he is not them. He is safe. But I think in the intimate relationships that have been already tested and proven to be safe places, the armor is less necessary.

—Ruthie Mengistu Williams

CREATING SPACE BETWEEN SELF AND ARMOR

Notice—Pause—Allow

Remember that your practice is to notice, pause, and allow what comes up to be there without judgment or shame. Let compassion, gratitude, and curiosity guide you as you use the following prompts and exercises to practice bringing awareness to your experience of the type structure. Below are some helpful ways to begin noticing the patterns of your type. The stress and security movements and somatic profile can help you begin to practice curiosity when you notice yourself showing up in these ways.

Stress and Security Movements

When Sixes are experiencing stress, they move toward Three. A conscious movement to Three can help Sixes move more quickly into action without getting stuck in analysis or overthinking. In this space, Sixes are more responsive to possibilities and can use their energy to achieve the necessary results. The unconscious movement to Three can be challenging for Sixes who don't typically operate with such a high bioenergetic charge. They might take on too much and experience burnout from overdoing while in the Three space.

When Sixes are relaxed and feel secure, they move toward the space of the Nine. A conscious movement to Nine helps Sixes relax into an acceptance of the present moment. They are able to broaden their thinking from just worst-case scenarios to see the whole picture. Their physical bodies are more relaxed and at ease. The challenge with an unconscious movement toward Nine is that Sixes might become inactive and unable to distinguish between options in order to make a decision.

Somatic Profile

Sixes have very sensitive nervous systems that are easily triggered by their environment. Imagine the flood of fear that would wash over your body if you were crossing the street and were almost hit by a car. For most of us, after the danger has passed, our bodies will return to homeostasis. For Sixes, their bodies live in this constant heightened state of fear. In some Sixes, their eyes might be guarded or distrusting, and these counterphobic Sixes tend to hold more of a rigid stance with a buildup of tension in their muscles. In other Sixes, their eyes might appear more fearful and protruding, and these phobic Sixes tend to withdraw into their heads or by physically leaving unsafe places.

Journal Prompts

Below are some prompts to help you begin to practice curiosity around the story of your type. Find a quiet place to reflect on these questions. Remember to be present with your body as you answer these prompts. Notice, pause, and allow. Be compassionate, curious, and grateful to your body for its intelligence. You can come back to this practice as often as you need to.

1. What is your earliest memory of feeling joyful and free? Where were you? Who were you with? What were you doing? Pause to check in: How does your body feel right now as you write about it?

2. What would change about the way you live if it were true that you have within you what it takes to thrive and that you can trust yourself? Pause to check in: How does your body feel right now as you write about it?

3. What if it's true that you can experience safety and security without life needing to be certain and predictable?

4. If you didn't *have* to be vigilant all the time, who would you be free to be?

5. When is your armor of vigilance necessary in your everyday life? When is it *not* necessary?

6. What does safety feel like in your body? Who do you feel safe with, enough to set down the armor? How does your body feel when you're with that person? Are you feeling some of that safety right now? You can always return to this space within yourself no matter what is happening outside of you.

Visualizations

Find a quiet place where you can relax without worry of interruption. If you are able, sit comfortably upright, uncrossing your hands and placing both feet flat on the floor. If you aren't able to do so, adjust your body to a position that helps you feel comfortable and grounded. Read through the prompt below, then close your eyes and begin to visualize. When you have completed the visualization, slowly bring your attention back to your body and the surface you are resting on, listen to the sounds around you, and open your eyes.

1. Visualize yourself picking up vigilance and putting it on like armor. What does your armor look like? How does your body feel when you are carrying the armor?
2. Visualize yourself taking off the armor of vigilance and setting it down. How does your body feel when you imagine setting down the armor in a safe space?

Community Practice

Often, we subconsciously weaponize our armor against others. If we live by a singular story, we try to subject others to that singular story as well. Because you believe you must be vigilant to be safe and secure, you might try to control others in an effort to keep them safe. Because you avoid uncertainty and unpredictability, you might demand more proof than others could possibly give in order to trust them. As you create space between yourself and your armor, I encourage you to consider how you require those around you to fit into your singular story. As you become more comfortable being with uncertainty, you will increase your capacity to make space for the uncertainty that is a natural part of life and relationships.

Chapter 15

TYPE FIVE: KNOWLEDGE AS ARMOR

NICKNAMES	The Observer, The Investigator
ARMOR	Knowledge
HOLY IDEA	Omniscience
VIRTUE/ESSENCE QUALITY	Nonattachment
MENTAL HABIT	Stinginess
EMOTIONAL HABIT	Avarice

HOLY IDEA

HOLY OMNISCIENCE: The River in Your Belly

I invite you to place your hand on your belly, particularly that space right beneath your belly button, and imagine that right there–inside of you–a deep river flows. This river holds all knowledge and carries within it sufficient energy for all that life requires. The river is both distinct from you and a part of you. This river is expansive, with a breadth and a depth so wide, you can't reach the end of it. When you drop down into this river in your belly, you are reminded that you have access to the knowledge and energy that is necessary to show up fully in each moment. There is always enough of whatever resources you need, generously offered to you by this river that doesn't run dry. You allow yourself to float in the river, entering its flow and letting it support and sustain you. When you are connected to this river, you know that it is impossible to reach a point of perpetual depletion because the river is always within you, full of the life-giving sustenance you need.

This is a depiction of **Holy Omniscience**, the objective reality, or Holy Idea, associated with the Type Five structure. Holy Omniscience is *a state of direct and transparent knowing that there is a flow of a universal energy that sustains you and meets real needs.* It invites us into a particular perception of reality, which reminds us that our connection to the flow gives us the capacity to bring our full attention and full presence to each moment without fear. Holy Omniscience reminds us that it is not on us individually to know it all or to gather all the resources we think will keep us safe. The knowledge and the resources we need in each moment are available to us when we are in the flow of the river.

When Fives are disconnected from Holy Omniscience, they come to believe that the world is a place in which too little is offered and too much is demanded of them. They forget that there is an infinite river that sustains them within, and they begin to believe that they must collect and hoard information and resources in order to keep themselves safe from the intrusive and overdemanding world. Because of this belief, they rarely show up fully in the present moment, afraid that it will demand too much of them and suck up their finite resources.

In reconnecting to Holy Omniscience, however, Fives exude the virtue of **nonattachment**. Nonattachment is an openhanded approach to life, a generosity of spirit in which their connection to the flow enables them to give of themselves and their energy without fear. Nonattachment helps Fives live generously, connected to experiential knowledge of the renewable nature of the resources we truly need to thrive. The invitation of this perspective on reality is to come back into oneself, to tap into the infinite flow that always exists, rather than using the mind as a way to combat the fear of not having enough.

IDEALIZATION

Knowledgeable, Self Sufficient

When a Five is disconnected from the objective reality of Holy Omniscience, they create a subjective story that says that the only way to ensure safety and security in a demanding and overwhelming world is to collect and hoard information, knowledge, and energy. As Head types, Fives use their minds to defend against their fears and procure security and safety. To combat the world and its seemingly endless demands on their time and energy, they become overly private, self-sufficient people.

Fives are naturally inquisitive, analytical, thoughtful, observant people. They enjoy learning and gathering information about topics that interest them, and they do this simply for the love of it. Their voracious minds are always hungry to learn more, understand more, know more. They tend to be good in a crisis because they are armed with all the information pertaining to that situation and how best to approach it. When the type structure is in the driver's seat, these attributes are co-opted in the service of an overarching story that says in an overwhelming and overdemanding world, knowledge is safety. Some Fives like to gather in-depth, thorough knowledge about a few topics that interest them the most, while others like to know a little bit about everything in addition to their primary interests. The main idea here is that the more information you have, the more self-sufficient and better insulated you can be from the demands of the world. The more you know, the less likely you are to be caught off guard.

Being knowledgeable means knowing all the angles and perspectives on a particular topic or as many angles or perspectives as I can get my hands on and being versed at explaining and talking about this. I'm okay personally with not knowing everything. But I would not put myself in a position where others would be looking to me for advice or for information if I don't know about something. I avoid not knowing by reading books and gathering information. Reading physical books is my preferred way of gathering information. Having a book allows me to scan through words and gather information quickly. Trying to gather information sent in video format just slows me down. Sometimes I do find myself in scenarios where you cannot know everything, and I have learned to be okay with that.

—Judith Lewis

Fives also believe they must be self-sufficient in order to remain safe in the world. Fives want to ensure that if being stranded on a desert island became a reality and not just an icebreaker question, they would be able to survive and keep themselves going without needing much. Because of this, Fives tend to limit their own desires and wants, believing that wanting less keeps them safe. They prefer lives of simplicity. Surviving on the bare minimum, whether that is with regard to affection, finances, or material conditions, allows the Five to live independent from others. The ultimate goal of self-sufficiency is to not have to depend on anyone else to be safe and secure. This is why Fives limit their desires and needs because often, those desires require a level of interdependency to be fulfilled.

This need to gather all the knowledge and resources needed to be self-sufficient and safe leads to a mental habit in Fives of **stinginess** or hoarding. Hoarding might make you think of those homes we see on TV that are packed to the brim with all sorts of knickknacks that the owner can't seem to part with. But for a Five who values simplicity, this hoarding is less about material acquisition and more about holding on to information, energy, and presence with a tight fist. Since Fives believe their safety and security lie in the amount of knowledge they have amassed, they find themselves being tightfisted with their information or resources in order to not run out.

The scarcity model undergirds this type structure. For Fives, the underlying belief is that there are just not enough resources for us all to thrive. Resources like time, energy, knowledge, and even affection are seen as finite and non-renewable, meaning that once you give them away, they are gone forever. This belief creates a mental pattern within Fives of hoarding their resources in order to remain safe against impending depletion. Fives believe it is their work of gathering and hoarding that enables their survival, forgetting that there is a universal flow that invites them to partake of the renewable resources that allow us to thrive.

AVOIDANCE

Not Knowing, Others' Demands, Intense Feelings

If you must be knowledgeable and self-sufficient in order to be safe, then not knowing is avoided at all costs. Since Fives' core story prioritizes knowledge or cognitive understanding over everything else, being in situations in which they don't know what to do or how to respond can bring up a sense of inner emptiness. It can feel like without knowledge, there is nothing substantial about them. To avoid this painful feeling of emptiness, Fives retract even further into their heads, blocking off access and connection to their hearts and bodies.

One of the aspects of life Fives tend to feel less knowledgeable about is the realm of feelings. Even though some Fives can appear factual and unemotional on the surface, they usually have a well of deep and intense feelings underneath the surface. They aren't sure how to engage with strong feelings both within themselves and from others, and so they avoid those feelings by retracting further into their heads to create distance between themselves and the intense feelings. To them, it can often seem like they are floating above reality—observing a situation from above without being fully present for it. For example, a close friend might be weeping in front of them, and they find that they are watching this happen from above the situation rather than from the ground. This allows them to detach themselves from their bodies and remain analytical and unaware of their own feelings, especially in situations that call for a more Heart-centered approach.

Fives are masters of the art of compartmentalized thinking. It's almost as if the mind of a Five is a well-organized storage room in which there are rows of clearly labeled filing cabinets. There is an assigned drawer for everything, and they can shut the drawers when they no longer wish to access the information stored there. This allows Fives to store away information and experiences in a way that helps them feel less overwhelmed. This compartmentalizing also happens in relationships. Fives can compartmentalize the way they show up with work friends versus with childhood friends versus with significant others versus with family. Knowing what is expected of them in each of these different relational arenas helps them feel safe. Most of the time, Fives try to keep these different groups of people from mixing because that would be the equivalent of someone running through their storage room and opening multiple drawers all at once. This, of course, would be stressful for Fives, and so they keep strict boundaries around their different relational circles.

Fives often experience the world around them as intrusive, and since they spend most of their time in their heads, someone interrupting the flow of their thoughts just to say hello could be experienced as an intrusion. They often experience others' relational requests as demands. A significant other requesting more time spent connecting can feel like a demand on their limited energy and time, which causes them to want to detach even further. Fives experience people as asking for too much and offering too little, but to actually receive the support and care that is available from others would require Fives to be present in their hearts and bodies. Since they work hard to stay only in their heads, they have limited access to be able to receive the support they need, and this keeps their idealized story going.

Having strong boundaries and being extremely private are other ways this type structure seeks to avoid not knowing and intense feelings or intrusion. Others might experience Fives as withdrawn or even reclusive. Fives often feel safest when they are alone or with one trusted other, and they organize their lives to ensure they have adequate alone time and space. When they are alone, there are no demands or intrusions, and there is no excessive emotional input from others, and this helps Fives restore their energy.

All these patterns of avoidance are fueled by a deep, core fear of **depletion**. With their scarcity mindset, Fives are afraid that if they don't work hard to preserve their reserves of energy, time, and knowledge, they will end up completely drained and without the resources needed to survive. If the world takes and takes without giving enough, they are afraid to let go of what they have for fear that it will never be replenished. This fear is what sustains the story that says, "*I must be knowledgeable and self-sufficient.*"

In my body, the fear of being depleted feels like an increase in heart rate. My mind is just really running, which I think causes the increase in the pulse. Since I just naturally enjoy being on my own, even from childhood, I didn't realize I was following a rule that had me protecting my energy. This fear also looks like me not wanting to be surprised, me wanting to be aware of any kind of social engagement that's coming up or knowing of any questions that will be asked of me ahead of time. I just don't want to be caught unexpected because if I know something is happening, I can plan for it mentally and have the space for it. Clarity is my thing. I like clarity on everything and from everyone who is interacting with me.

—Judith Lewis

DEFENSE MECHANISM

Isolation

For a Five, the best way to avoid intrusion, strong feelings, and not knowing enough is to isolate yourself from both the outside world and your body and emotions. Another word for this defense mechanism is detachment, and both words highlight the Five's defense of remaining aloof in order to stay protected from being depleted. Sometimes, Fives detach by physically going away and keeping to themselves or choosing to not show up for certain events or situations that would overwhelm and deplete them. For example, in a social setting, a Five might retreat to the bathroom for a significant amount of time to recover from the social demands and be able to return to the group.

But Fives can also detach without moving their physical bodies. Those in relationships with Fives know the telltale sign of a Five disappearing into their head even while they remain seated or standing in front of you. It's like their eyes glaze over, and the person speaking to them can tell that the Five has left the conversation. In our very digital world, maybe Fives stay in the room but get on their phones, reading articles and watching videos while conversations go on around them. In relational conflict, unsure of how to recognize what they are feeling, Fives detach into their minds and turn to analysis and facts as a way to dampen the intensity of the feelings. Of course, a lot of times this leads whoever they're in conflict with to intensify their own reactions because they experience Fives as aloof and emotionally disconnected. This is a depiction of the emotional habit of Fives, which is called **avarice** but is better understood as a withholding of self. Remember that the belief here is that if you give too much of yourself away, you will end up depleted. As protection against that, Fives withhold themselves from the people in their lives who they believe will take and take and never give enough to replenish.

As mentioned before, Fives feel deeply but rarely show that on the surface. When Fives are alone, they tend to return to emotionally intense situations to process and parse out their own experiences. Maybe in the conflict mentioned above, the Five feels hurt or betrayed. In the moment, the type structure keeps the Five floating above reality, only responding with mental analysis for their safety. When they are alone afterward, they might feel freer to return to the scenario they observed from above and notice their feelings of hurt and betrayal. Since this type is overly concerned with self-sufficiency, however, Fives don't tend to self-disclose their innermost feelings, even after they have become aware of them. Disclosing their feelings and inviting in the support of others would introduce the kind of dependency that registers as unsafe within the mind of the Five. They might think, *"If I become dependent on their care or support and it goes away, I won't have what I need to survive, so it's best to take care of it myself."* Unfortunately for a Five, taking care of their emotional needs often means simply filing the need away in its appropriate folder and shutting the drawer.

Sometimes being present in our hearts and bodies can be overwhelming, this is true. And while the hoarding of resources might help us survive, thriving requires us to be in the flow of the present moment, not detached from it. Although Fives work so hard to protect their energy by detaching, it actually takes more energy to keep yourself floating above reality than to simply be present. When Fives practice presence, they rediscover that river within, which offers them more access to the experiential knowledge that there is a natural flow and supply of the energy, resources, and nurturance necessary for a thriving life.

In some ways, my knowledge is what I can rely on, being a manager of my organization where I am a woman with a small build and generally on the quieter end of things. So when I show up in board meetings, and people generally think I'm ten years younger than I really am, I lean on knowledge as a way of proving who I am and building trust. This is where I think my armor of knowledge is necessary.

But there are also times when I'm completely okay with not being the person that has all the answers. I almost intentionally don't want to train people to think that they can come to me because I know everything. I've found out that even when I know a lot, I don't know everything. So I embrace that and try to create a culture of interacting with people so they know that I will tell them what I think but that it's not everything.

Fives tend to delay action while they seek knowledge, or they think the seeking of knowledge is, in fact, action. I am learning to differentiate between the two things and allow myself to take real action, not just research, even when I don't know everything about that particular situation or I don't have everything prepared. For me, I don't know if the emphasis is on knowledge as much as it is competency. I know that there is no limit or end to knowledge, so I just seek enough knowledge to be competent at what I'm being asked to do.

—Judith Lewis

CREATING SPACE BETWEEN SELF AND ARMOR

Notice—Pause—Allow

Remember that your practice is to notice, pause, and allow what comes up to be there without judgment or shame. Let compassion, gratitude, and curiosity guide you as you use the following prompts and exercises to practice bringing awareness to your experience of the type structure. Below are some helpful ways to begin noticing the patterns of your type. The stress and security movements and somatic profile can help you begin to practice curiosity when you notice yourself showing up in these ways.

Stress and Security Movements

When Fives are experiencing stress, they move toward Seven. A conscious movement to Seven can help Fives show up with more energy and enthusiasm. They have access to a more sociable side of themselves, and in this space, they might even show up as the life of the party. The unconscious movement to Seven can be challenging for Fives if they engage in escapism as a way to deal with feeling overwhelmed. A Five might overspend or overindulge in order to feel okay.

When Fives are relaxed and feel secure, they move toward the space of the Eight. A conscious movement to Eight helps a Five gain access to the vitality and groundedness of the Body Center. In this space, Fives are connected to the energy of their bodies and utilize that energy to assertively move into action. The challenge with an unconscious movement toward Eight is that Fives might come across as excessively forceful in their attempts to get their point across. Others might experience them as more concerned with asserting their positions than the unpleasant impact doing so might have on others.

Somatic Profile

In Fives, energy is withdrawn from other parts of the body and concentrated in the core. When a Five feels tension, it is often in their gut. Fives tend to be very sensitive to external stimuli, like touch and sound, and can find these things intrusive to their internal experience. It can be easy to tell when a Five has withdrawn through their eyes, as they tend to get a glassed-over look that indicates they are no longer attending to the present moment.

Journal Prompts

Below are some prompts to help you begin to practice curiosity around the story of your type. Find a quiet place to reflect on these questions. Remember to be present with your body as you answer these prompts. Notice, pause, and allow. Be compassionate, curious, and grateful to your body for its intelligence. You can come back to this practice as often as you need to.

1. What is your earliest memory of feeling joyful and free? Where were you? Who were you with? What were you doing? Pause to check in: How does your body feel right now as you write about it?
2. What would change about the way you live if it were true that there is an infinite supply of the resources and energy you need to thrive? Pause to check in: How does your body feel right now as you write about it?
3. What if it's true that you can experience safety and security without having all the knowledge and facts?
4. If you didn't *have* to be knowledgeable all the time, who would you be free to be?
5. When is your armor of knowledge necessary in your everyday life? When is it *not* necessary?
6. What does safety feel like in your body? Who do you feel safe with, enough to set down the armor? How does your body feel when you're with that person? Are you feeling some of that safety right now? You can

always return to this space within yourself no matter what is happening outside of you.

Visualizations

Find a quiet place where you can relax without worry of interruption. If you are able, sit comfortably upright, uncrossing your hands and placing both feet flat on the floor. If you aren't able to do so, adjust your body to a position that helps you feel comfortable and grounded. Read through the prompt below, then close your eyes and begin to visualize. When you have completed the visualization, slowly bring your attention back to your body and the surface you are resting on, listen to the sounds around you, and open your eyes.

1. Visualize yourself picking up knowledge and putting it on like armor. What does your armor look like? How does your body feel when you are carrying the armor?
2. Visualize yourself taking off the armor of knowledge and setting it down. How does your body feel when you imagine setting down the armor in a safe space?

Community Practice

Often, we subconsciously weaponize our armor against others. If we live by a singular story, we try to subject others to that singular story as well. Because you believe you must be knowledgeable to be safe and secure, you might dismiss people who value other ways of knowing or who prioritize intelligence from the heart and body. Because you avoid not knowing and intense feelings, you might withdraw when you feel incompetent, leaving others feeling rejected. As you create space between yourself and your armor, I encourage you to consider how you require those around you to fit into your singular story. As you become more comfortable showing up even when you don't have all the answers, you will increase your capacity for connection and receptivity.

Chapter 16

TYPE SEVEN: OPTIMISM AS ARMOR

NICKNAMES	The Epicure, The Enthusiast
ARMOR	Optimism
HOLY IDEA	Work
VIRTUE/ESSENCE QUALITY	Constancy
MENTAL HABIT	Planning
EMOTIONAL HABIT	Gluttony

HOLY IDEA

HOLY WORK: The Sushi Carousel

In certain sushi restaurants, customers sit around a giant sushi carousel in the middle of the restaurant. While you're at your table, expertly crafted and plated sushi comes drifting by on the conveyor belt, and when you see a plate you want, you grab it off the belt. Let's imagine that you're sitting at one of those restaurants enjoying your sushi. There's no need to worry about whether there will be enough sushi or if you will leave satisfied. You can stay and eat as much as you'd like, knowing that there is a team of people in the back with a plan to keep the sushi plates coming out consistently. You can trust that what you need will come your way without you needing to plan for it. Your work, then, is to sit and savor what is right in front of you, to let yourself really taste and fully enjoy the sushi that's already on your plate. When your plate is empty, you can look to the carousel for what comes next.

This is a depiction of **Holy Work**, the objective reality, or Holy Idea, associated with the Type Seven structure. Holy Work is a *state of focused concentration that allows you to travel the full spectrum of life fully and freely*. Holy Work says that there is a *wisdom* to the unfolding of life, and within that wisdom there is a *plan* that includes you and your well-being. When you are able to trust this wisdom is already at work, you experience the freedom to bring focused attention to what is truly your work. Real work can only be done in the present moment, not the future or the past. This Holy Idea brings to mind one of my favorite Mary Oliver poems in which she writes: "Let me keep my mind on what matters, / which is my work, / which is mostly standing still and learning to be astonished."

When a Seven is disconnected from this objective reality, they begin to feel afraid that the sushi might run out or that the chef might not make enough of their favorite roll or that others will grab more than their fair share, leaving the

Seven enduring an unpleasant experience. The Seven then sees their work as keeping an eye on the carousel to make sure they don't miss out, meanwhile missing out on being fully present to the sushi that's already on their plate. By trying to avoid future hunger and disappointment, they miss the opportunity to satiate their present hunger with what's already been given to them.

This is why trust is such an important component of this Holy Idea. When a Seven can trust that there is a plan at work to satisfy their real needs, they can bring their attention back to the present moment. When a Seven is able to trust the wisdom and plan at work, and therefore focus on their own work, they exude the virtue of **constancy**, which is the ability to stay present to the experience of the full spectrum of life. Rather than leaving the present moment to try and curate future satisfaction, constancy allows the Seven to experience the satisfaction and contentedness that is only found in the present moment. Real work can only be done in the present moment. This is the reminder for Sevens and for all of us.

IDEALIZATION

Optimistic, Upbeat

When a Seven is disconnected from the objective reality of Holy Work, they create a subjective story that says that the best way to ensure their security and safety is through keeping life optimistic and full of possibilities. Sevens are naturally enthusiastic, energetic, fun people who curate lives filled with excitement and pleasure. They are the ones you go to if you want to have a good time, whether that be a wild night on the town, a spontaneous trip, or a well-curated dinner party at home. Sevens tend to be spontaneous people, always on the hunt for the next exciting adventure. They bring their childlike enthusiasm and zest for life to whatever they do. At their best, Sevens invite us all to see what is possible and to chase those possibilities with excitement.

When the type structure is in the driver's seat, it contracts these naturally optimistic tendencies into a singular story that says, *"You* must *be optimistic and keep life positive or you will no longer be safe and secure."* Sevens believe it is their optimism and their natural ability to find and create possibilities that ensures that they have access to safety and security. Whenever they encounter a difficulty or inconvenience, they are skilled at looking for what positivity can be gleaned from the difficulty. I heard it described once as Sevens walking around with a pocket full of silver linings, ready to throw at any clouds they encounter. Silver linings can sound like: *"Well, at least . . ."* or *"But on the bright side . . ."* or *"It could be worse."* This pattern of behavior serves to keep the attention of the Seven focused only on what they want to see.

Sevens are constantly on the move, whether literally or in the constant motion of their minds. Their minds have the incredible capacity of following multiple threads of thought simultaneously and somehow finding a way to weave those seemingly unrelated thoughts together. To those in conversation with them, it might seem as though they are constantly distracted and unable to focus. But within the mind of the Seven, all the rabbit trails are connected in some way. Often this constant motion serves as a way to keep the Seven from feeling stuck or from missing out on what else could be out there.

For Sevens, safety and security are synonymous with freedom. Feeling the freedom to explore, be adventurous, and keep their options open is imperative for this type. Anything that hampers that sense of freedom is avoided at all costs. But if your freedom requires constant movement—always in forward motion to avoid what might be difficult in the present moment—are you really free? Chances are, if you cannot be still and still be free, then your "freedom" is really just escapism.

Sevens truly believe that pain can be avoided. Part of the internal belief system of this type is that life limits us and causes unnecessary pain that can be avoided. For the Seven, the need to avoid pain and secure happiness creates a mental habit of **planning**. Planning for the future, for possibilities, and for adventures keeps the mind of the Seven occupied with the future at the expense of fully experiencing the present. A Seven is the type most likely to be planning their next vacation while currently on vacation. Planning gives their busy mind something to do, but it also helps keep their fears at bay. Having a plan gives you a sense of assurance that you will be safe from pain, even if you cannot know this for sure.

> A big part of optimism for me is being detached from the heart or emotions. There's a mental fascination with being able to look forward to the future, to plan or create something in the future. What I've come to realize now is that optimism is more of a faux version of happiness or joy. It's being buzzy, overly comical, flipping everything to make it positive. With anything and everything that could be negative, I flip the situation and then take pride in it. That's the scary part too—taking pride in it.
>
> —Milton Stewart

AVOIDANCE

Pain, Suffering, Limitations

To keep life optimistic and full of possibilities, Sevens avoid anything that feels like pain, suffering, or limitations. I asked a friend who identifies as a Seven recently what it's like for her to experience limitations. Her entire body shuddered and spasmed as if I had just said the most vile, offensive thing. She said with emphasis, "I *hate* limitations." This is a common sentiment for type Sevens, who curate their lives in order to avoid being limited in any way.

Limitations for a Seven could be anything from being given a structure and guidelines for how to work on a project to committing to a plan too far in advance. They will likely disregard your structure but still get you the deliverables you want and might be noncommittal about your invitation in order to keep their options open. If a limitation cannot be avoided completely, Sevens will work around it to make it feel less limiting.

The same is true for the experiences of pain and suffering. In order to keep life optimistic and positive, pain is either avoided or made more palatable by throwing a silver lining on it. Sevens react the same way to their own pain as well as to the pain of others. They have a tendency toward intellectualizing pain, which enables them to talk about a difficult experience without having to actually be present with it in their hearts and bodies.

To avoid pain or limitations, a part of me just doesn't acknowledge that limitations even exist. Until my body experiences them, and then there's a whole different thing that happens. Another way I avoid pain, especially emotional pain, is through food. Pleasure is a huge thing for me, so using any form of pleasure to deal with emotional pain has been my track record. As a self-preservation Seven, I love to be comfortable, and anything I can do to be comfortable, I will buy it or go do it. A subtle strategy that I've noticed is that I use this funny laugh and smile to make things feel light. But that's actually defensive. That's me trying not to go there if there's pain or limitations.

—Milton Stewart

Sevens feel frustrated when it seems to them like others are "stuck" in their pain, and the type structure kicks into overdrive in their attempts to get others to transcend their pain quickly. A little bit of pain is okay; most people recognize that life isn't always ideally how we want it to be. But the fear here is more about the feeling of being stuck, of being trapped in something painful or limiting with no way out. The core fear of Sevens is **deprivation**. At their core, Sevens are terrified that if they allow themselves to dip their toes into the pool of pain or limitations, they will be sucked in and trapped down there forever, unable to come up for air. And in that stuck, trapped place, they will be deprived of all of the goodness, pleasure, and possibility life has to offer. To make sure this doesn't happen they dance around the pool, careful to not get too close to the water in case they fall in and get trapped.

The fear of being trapped and deprived shows up in my body. It's almost like all the blood in my body speeds up, like everything in my body wants to go faster. It wants to move and do something. It's like, "Let's find a way to be stimulated because we cannot be stuck in this." I actually struggle with that on both bad things *and* good things. If I've done a wonderful job of doing something, usually there are emotions of gratitude, and there's a deep sense of love and real excitement from it. Internally, there is an aversion in my body to feeling that. Everything speeds up so I can be more stimulated and I don't have to deal with the gravity of those good feelings. I'm not able to fully process the feelings.

I've actually been able to feel the lower or negative emotions a little bit more than the happy ones, like real joy. When I'm experiencing true joy, my heart is warm, tender. My emotions, my head, and my body are one. It's like they're all in the same room hanging out together and having such a good time, and things slow down. I speak and I move slower to a certain degree. And I feel connected, like this deep, rich connection that's just warm. Usually I feel more electrical, buzzy energy, but joy is a warm, grounded feeling, and it just is very pleasant. Once I recognized and felt real joy, the fake version doesn't do it for me anymore.

—Milton Stewart

For many of the Sevens I've worked with, what has stood out to me is a common experience in childhood of aloneness in the midst of a painful or distressing situation. Whether it was the unexpected news of their parents' divorce or a tragic death, the little Seven felt distress and, for whatever reason, didn't get the support and soothing they needed from the adults. That experience of feeling trapped in a painful situation that made no sense to you as a little kid is what motivates this type structure to curate life with the goal of never having to feel that trapped and alone again. The pain, and the aloneness with the pain, is too much to bear, so Sevens focus on fun ways to distract themselves from the pain, patterns of thinking that make situations more bearable. This pattern of self-protective avoidance repeats itself over and over again until it becomes embedded in their personalities.

DEFENSE MECHANISM

Rationalization

As Head types, Sevens use the power of their minds to defend themselves against the painful realities of life. The defense mechanism of rationalization helps them avoid being trapped in limitations and pain while maintaining a positive outlook. Rationalization refers to the habitual pattern of explaining away painful or distressing experiences in order to keep the focus on what is positive or possible. We all rationalize bad situations, but if rationalization was a sport, Sevens would win the Olympic gold medals every time.

The metaphor of having a pocket full of silver linings to throw at every cloud is a perfect depiction of rationalization. The minds of Sevens are primed to breeze over the difficulty or pain while reminding themselves and others to "look on the bright side!" As we explored in the previous section, Sevens do this because of their fear of being stuck in pain and deprived of goodness. In our society that thrives on toxic positivity and a "good vibes only" mentality, rationalization is often praised as an excellent skill to possess. Anything that keeps us focused on the positive is good, right?

But what we lose when we elevate positivity over everything is contact with our full humanity and the full humanity of others. There is so much more to the human experience, and just because we ignore certain parts of that experience doesn't mean they go away. Sevens are terrified of not experiencing the fullness of life, and they want to curate their lives as much as possible to ensure they aren't deprived of all the new and exciting experiences life has to offer. In striving to curate life only for the high side, Sevens end up missing out on the full spectrum of life. Sevens don't want to feel trapped in limitations and deprived of the fullness of life. And yet the type structure's patterns limit their ability to be present with an open heart to the fullness of life. While they are afraid of missing out on the high side of life, they end up missing out on everything else their type structure works to avoid.

Gluttony is the emotional habit of this type and refers to the desire for more novelty, more pleasure, more fun, more of the best the world and its people have to offer. But gluttony can't really be satiated because it is not focused on meeting a real need. Rather, the focus is on excess, a perpetual desire for more that leads to overconsumption. If the goal is to always be searching for more, satisfaction can never be experienced because what you already have will never be enough.

This habit of gluttony is also a trap that often creates more of the pain or suffering Sevens think they are avoiding. For example, having too many options or too many fun plans on the calendar can lead to a Seven feeling overwhelmed, anxious, and even trapped in the decision-making process about what to prioritize.

I think about Black culture in the United States as a predominantly Seven culture. There is so much pain, grief, loss, and trauma embedded in the experience of being Black in this country that the possibility of drowning in the pool of pain feels very real. It isn't just old pain or unprocessed trauma from childhood; it is a near-constant reminder that we are not safe or valued in this white supremacist system. So what do Black folks do, and do extremely well? We use humor to cope. We share memes and laugh, we turn up, we distract ourselves and keep things light in an effort to not break open completely from the grief. For us, the armor of the Seven is completely necessary because the pain is inflicted on a constant basis, and we need a reprieve so that we don't sink into hopelessness.

The reminder for Sevens and for all of us is that the armor is only a one-sided story of who we are. While we hold the incredible capacity for joy in the midst of despair, grief can also be a teacher. Learning to be present with our experiences of grief, limitations, pain, and suffering can help our bodies process and release those emotions. When we don't do that, they become trapped inside of us and come out sideways in other damaging behavior. While we cannot curate our lives to be devoid of pain like the Seven desperately wants to do, we can learn how to be with our pain in a way that helps us become freer and more open.

If I didn't have to be optimistic all the time, interestingly enough, I'd be free to be me. I think when I go places, people are used to seeing me be upbeat and happy and bring energy. It took me a while to realize that I am not okay all the time. Unconsciously I believed that I was okay, even though there's a part of me that's like, "Oh, I don't feel good." I never registered that. Realizing that I wasn't okay messed me up. If I didn't have to be optimistic all the time, I would actually be free to not be okay. I would be free to be me in totality. Especially as a Black man, I do feel like I put on a lot of times in circles and places for multiple reasons, especially safety. Safety is huge. But I think if I didn't have to be optimistic, I'd be fully me. And that means to allow myself the range of emotions, allow myself to be with my heart, in circles with other people, and not flee from it or distract them and/or myself from actually being able to be in touch with my heart, which really connects me. But it's tricky to go there.

My armor of optimism is necessary in everyday life when I enter situations where there is no moving forward unless you are optimistic. I think it's also necessary to have it even in situations that may get very intense or tense in a way that people may not feel safe. Being able to bring the armor of optimism, to a certain degree, allows people to feel a little bit safer, to relax tensions, and to connect people through laughter or through energy that's a little bit higher than what they brought or what's in the room. When I step outside of my house, my comfort zone, and I see different people who could potentially harm me as a Black man, my body automatically tightens up. My solar plexus is where it becomes the tightest and feels a little suffocating. When I'm interacting with cops, I feel like wearing glasses when I drive and being able to vibrate at a higher frequency with energy that is lighter disarms certain cops who will see me as a threat. I feel like that's when the armor is heavily needed. Because if I respond in any other way than my type structure, who knows what could happen?

When it's not needed is when I'm really with people who love and care for me, and I feel it. I had to recognize that the people I've assembled around me that I do care about and trust—they trust and care about me too. I had to realize that if I put them in my stratosphere, then they're probably pretty trustworthy, and I can give them a little bit more of myself. I can actually lay down the shields and experience a lightness there. Not a Seven lightness where my legs become real light and I'm not grounded, but a lightness in the chest and the heart area where I don't have to carry as much. I can literally just be. That's very seldom and rare that I feel that, but when I am around people who, it don't matter what you do, the unconditional love is really there. Those are moments where I feel that lightness.

—Milton Stewart

CREATING SPACE BETWEEN SELF AND ARMOR

Notice—Pause—Allow

Remember that your practice is to notice, pause, and allow what comes up to be there without judgment or shame. Let compassion, gratitude, and curiosity guide you as you use the following prompts and exercises to practice bringing awareness to your experience of the type structure. Below are some helpful ways to begin noticing the patterns of your type. The stress and security movements and somatic profile can help you begin to practice curiosity when you notice yourself showing up in these ways.

Stress and Security Movements

When Sevens are experiencing stress, they move toward One. A conscious movement to One can help Sevens structure their boundless energy into practical action. At One, Sevens are able to be more organized, responsible, and orderly. The unconscious movement to One can be challenging for Sevens as they might become critical and judgmental of self and others, demanding that things be done perfectly or the right way. They might become resentful of others who aren't doing things right.

When Sevens are relaxed and feel secure, they move toward the space of the Five. A conscious movement to Five helps a Seven find their center. Here, Sevens are able to go inward in quiet reflection, stilling the quick pace of their mental activity and stimulation in order to find clarity and peace. The challenge with an unconscious movement toward Five is that it might feel lonely or boring to be so quiet and reflective. In this quiet space, they might become more aware of their fear, which can be uncomfortable for Sevens to be present with.

Somatic Profile

Sevens hold their energy in the body's periphery—arms, legs—and away from their core. The strategy here is to disperse the energy through constant stimulation, whether through adventures, substances, or ideas. Rather than hold rigidity or physical tension in their bodies, they avoid painful feelings by going into their minds. By staying in their heads and their bodies' periphery, they are able to keep their bodies light, with energy going up and out.

Journal Prompts

Below are some prompts to help you begin to practice curiosity around the story of your type. Find a quiet place to reflect on these questions. Remember to be present with your body as you answer these prompts. Notice, pause, and allow. Be compassionate, curious, and grateful to your body for its intelligence. You can come back to this practice as often as you need to.

1. What is your earliest memory of feeling joyful and free? Where were you? Who were you with? What were you doing? Pause to check in: How does your body feel right now as you write about it?
2. What would change about the way you live if it were true that there is a universal wisdom that you can trust

to sustain and support your well-being? Pause to check in: How does your body feel right now as you write about it?

3. What if it's true that you can access safety and security in your body without needing to escape the present moment or experiences of pain?

4. If you didn't *have* to be optimistic all the time, who would you be free to be?

5. When is your armor of optimism necessary in your everyday life? When is it *not* necessary?

6. What does safety feel like in your body? Who do you feel safe with, enough to set down the armor? How does your body feel when you're with that person? Are you feeling some of that safety right now? You can always return to this space within yourself no matter what is happening outside of you.

Visualizations

Find a quiet place where you can relax without worry of interruption. If you are able, sit comfortably upright, uncrossing your hands and placing both feet flat on the floor. If you aren't able to do so, adjust your body to a position that helps you feel comfortable and grounded. Read through the prompt below, then close your eyes and begin to visualize. When you have completed the visualization, slowly bring your attention back to your body and the surface you are resting on, listen to the sounds around you, and open your eyes.

1. Visualize yourself picking up optimism and putting it on like armor. What does your armor look like? How does your body feel when you are carrying the armor?
2. Visualize yourself taking off the armor of optimism and setting it down. How does your body feel when you imagine setting down the armor in a safe space?

Community Practice

Often, we subconsciously weaponize our armor against others. If we live by a singular story, we try to subject others to that singular story as well. Because you believe you must be optimistic to be safe and secure, you might try to enforce your optimistic view on others around you or see yourself as superior to those you deem less optimistic. Because you avoid pain and limitations, you might diminish or trivialize the pain of others because of your own discomfort. As you create space between yourself and your armor, I encourage you to consider how you require those around you to fit into your singular story. As you become more comfortable with experiences of pain and limitations, you will increase your capacity to be more supportive with the pain of others.

CONCLUSION

Our Enneagram types can serve as necessary armor in a world that is still inequitable and unjust. Our bodies bear the brunt of that inequity and deserve our protection. Yet our bodies also hold memories of the full selves beneath our woundedness and beneath our armor, the selves that have greater access to the expansive reality in which we know we are deserving of love, care, safety, worth, and belonging. Our bodies can be access points for safety and rest, no matter what is happening around us.

My hope is that the exploration of Enneagram types in this way allows you to see that you are not just the things you've learned to do to survive. I hope you are able to hold the awareness of your armor with compassion and grace, not shame. And I hope you take with you the reminder that we are more than the struggle and more than our armor. The main thing is to not confuse the armor with the fullness of who we are, to practice daily creating that space between armor and self so that we can access the freedom, joy, love, and care that we are always deserving of, no matter what. This allows us to show up from a place of worthiness and enoughness rather than a place of striving or control or incessant fighting. We can still find rest and thrive, not just in a future, more equitable world, but right here and right now.

We've explored how we are often subconsciously led by the avoidance of our fears in our daily lives and the nine ways in which those patterns of avoidance help create our armor. But what if we lived more from the space of what we desire and what we love? What if we moved toward what is easeful, restful, and pleasurable rather than simply the avoidance of pain? If we lived desire-first, who would we be? What would we create? How would we spend our days? How would we choose to show up?

As Black folks, we can spend so much of our time arguing with folks who are committed to not seeing us as deserving regardless of the eloquence of our arguments or the force of our rage. What if we centered our softness, our ease, our joy, our love? It certainly wouldn't make the world magically better or eliminate all the threats to our well-being, but it would create space within us to see ourselves in the fullness of our glory and not just through the lens of the world's stories about us. In a world that requires us to stay hardened, tough, impenetrable, and compliant, centering ease and joy and love allows us to reconnect with our freer inner children who know how to play and delight in themselves and others.

In the summer of 2020, a viral tweet from a Black man who said he had just frolicked for the first time ever was shared around the internet. He posted pictures of himself lying down, jumping, and dancing in a field. It spurred many videos in response of Black people running around fields and frolicking with ease. That visual is what I want for us collectively: the freedom to frolic, to play, to experience joy—and not the escapism of our collective Seven-ness but a true grounded joy—to experience ease and rest even while the world is still a mess. So, in parting, here is my love letter to all nine types:

Nines, you are easy to love, not because you shrink yourself into palatable containers but because the fullness of who you are when you allow it to be seen is beautiful. You don't have to earn your place at the table; you don't have to be a smaller version of yourself to belong. There is enough space for you to bring all of who you are to the table. The fullness of who you are is easy to love.

Ones, your imperfections are what make you easy to love. There is so much beauty and goodness that resides in you just as you are, without you needing to change a thing. Every mistake and imperfection creates a container into which love, grace, and acceptance can be poured. You are free to exist as whole and worthy and imperfect and still loved.

Twos, letting others love you and show up for your needs is the real gift. You don't need to be the river that sustains everyone around you. Owning your needs allows space for you to receive all the love that you have always been deserving of. You don't need to work hard to earn love and acceptance; who you are when you aren't doing is already enough.

Threes, your value isn't tied to what you can produce. Applause is nice, but it doesn't determine your value. You don't have to perform for love. You are free to pause, to remember how to enjoy being without having to do all of the time. You could fail at every single thing you attempt to do and still be deserving of love. Who you are, separate from all the roles you play, is whole and worthy of being seen and loved.

Fours, your sameness and mundaneness is just as lovable as your uniqueness. You don't need to stand out to be deserving of attention and love. You don't have to wait for other people to offer you value or invite you into connection. You have always been deserving of love without effort, just as you are, without any performance. Don't abandon yourself for the validation of others.

Fives, your presence is a gift to yourself and others around you. There is more access to replenishment when you're in the flow of the present moment, not detached from it. Love, care, and energy are renewable resources. You can ask for the love and care you need because there is enough. You won't run out of what you need to thrive, but you have to come down into the present, into your body, into that river in your belly to access the resources that are always there for you.

Sixes, you can trust yourself. You can trust that your wisdom and intuition can guide you through the uncertainties of life. You deserve to experience the fullness of reality, including what is light, easy, healing, and fun. Your preparedness will not eliminate the uncertainties of life, but your intuition can guide you moment by moment into the next right thing. You deserve to experience ease even while life continues to be uncertain.

Sevens, you don't always have to be a buoy, fighting to remain on the surface of the water. You can be an anchor, connected to the ground yet still fluid and free. You can travel the spectrum from surface to depth freely because you are supported by love. You are not required to brighten every dark room or lighten every load. You don't have to always be okay. You are free to allow yourself to not be okay and to receive the support and love that is available for you.

Eights, the essence of who you are is inherently good. Your vulnerabilities and weaknesses make space for you to receive love and care. You don't have to be strong enough to handle it all; your strength doesn't make you more worthy of belonging. You are free to be all of who you are—tender, capable, scared, hopeful, weak, assertive, receptive, loud, quiet, soft, strong. The entirety of who you are is worthy of belonging.

And a reminder for every person, no matter what type you identify with: you are enough; you are worthy; you are loved.

ACKNOWLEDGMENTS

To the entire team at Broadleaf Books and particularly my editor, Lisa Kloskin, who believed in the possibility of this book right from the start—thank you for believing in me without proof that I could really do this! Your direct and kind feedback made this process a dream come true.

To my teachers at the Narrative Enneagram from whom I learned so much about not just this system but also how to embody integration—thank you for the wisdom, presence, and compassion you offered me throughout my journey. This book wouldn't exist without you. In particular, thank you to Renée Rosario who has been my mentor and advocate—I hope this book makes you proud.

To my early readers who read through the very first draft and offered feedback that helped shape this final version—Annie, Cassie, Grace, Kailin—thank you for being so generous with your time and energy.

To Abi Robins, who walked through the door and held it open for me to enter, thank you for introducing me to Lisa and kick-starting this process! I'm excited for our books to live on shelves next to each other.

To my family of friends whose love sustains me—thank you for always being a safe place for me to let out the playful (aka truest) version of myself. When I'm with you, I feel like who I am is always enough, and that is the greatest gift. Grace, thank you for the constant encouragement and support in the last few weeks of writing this manuscript and for transcribing the stories people shared for the book. Kailin, thank you for everything, especially celebrating every single win of mine like it's your own. Cassie, thank you for being my writing partner. Writing with you made me better. My Circle of Straight Oxygen, thank you for the clutch-your-sides laughter every time we're together. Laugh-crying with you made 2020-21 (and writing a book about liberation in 2020-21) bearable.

To my therapist, my unicorn, Melody, thank you for getting me together so often, for reflecting my light back to me when I doubt it, for believing in my life's work and offering your always-on-point guidance.

To my queen mother, the definition of elegance, integrity, and strength—every wonderful thing about me today started as a seed you planted. Thank you for telling me so often how proud you are of me, for encouraging my love of words and books since childhood, for instilling a love of learning in me. I did it, Mom! I'm a published author!

To the Divine, thank you for placing this gift within me. I hope to keep learning how to use it well.

RESOURCES

Healing and liberation work is collective work, as we explored at the very beginning of this book. In the same way, using the Enneagram as a tool for liberation requires a community lens and practice. We need people to learn with and from, people to help us see when we are trapped in our singular stories or overidentifying with our armor, people to remind us of our inherent dignity and worthiness when we forget. We heal together, and we get free together. I've included a list of resources that include coaches and groups that can support your continued journey with the Enneagram. If you are unsure still of what your type is, a typing interview with a trained Enneagram professional can help you explore your particular patterns and habits related to type structure.

Finally, there is so much more to explore within the system of the Enneagram, like our instincts and subtypes (where our energy habitually goes on a daily basis and the stage on which the drama of our emotional habits plays out). We could explore relational dynamics, conflict resolution styles, intimacy, and so much more. The focus of this book, though, was to offer a different context in which the discussion around our types and growth work could be held. There are many books already that offer incredible guidance around these other topics, and you will find a short list of my favorites below.

COACHES

Jessica Denise Dickson: https://jessicaddickson.com
Milton Stewart: https://www.kaizencareers.com

WOC SUPPORT GROUPS/COHORTS

Tracey Gee: https://www.instagram.com/traceygee.me/
The Black Enneagram: https://www.instagram.com/the
blackenneagram/
Enneagram in Color: https://www.instagram.com/ennea
gramincolor/

SCHOOLS

The Narrative Enneagram: https://www.narrativeennea
gram.org
The Enneagram Institute: https://www.enneagraminsti
tute.com

BOOKS

The Essential Enneagram: The Definitive Personality Test and Self-Discovery Guide, David Daniels and Virginia Price

The Enneagram in Love & Work: Understanding Your Intimate & Business Relationships, Helen Palmer

The Spiritual Dimension of the Enneagram: Nine Faces of the Soul, Sandra Maitri

The Complete Enneagram: 27 Paths to Greater Self-Knowledge, Beatrice Chestnut

The Conscious Enneagram: How to Move from Typology to Transformation, Abi Robins

A GUIDE TO PRACTICING FREEDOM

In my work with Black women one-on-one and in groups, a conversation comes up frequently around what it means for Black women in particular to be free, to be at ease, and to experience liberation. There is a lot of pushback around the idea. We Black folks often feel like our lived experiences and daily stressors don't allow space for ease, freedom, and rest.

I completely get it. There is so much that we have to constantly be guarded against or fight against. The overwhelming amount of regular incoming threats can make joy, ease, and freedom feel inaccessible for us. Freedom starts to feel like a luxury for those who don't have to face the constant barrage of oppression, systemic inequities, and things that are trying to harm and kill us.

What I realized in these conversations is that many of us think about freedom and liberation in a very limited way. How we think about what it means for us to be free or what a free version of ourselves would be like is still bound within the limited imagination of systems of supremacy. How we do one thing is how we do everything, so because we face so many limitations to our full expression of freedom, even our *imagination* of freedom has become limited. The pushback I encounter stems from this idea that freedom looks like having the ability to coast without a single worry or care in the world, having access to all the money you could ever want, and not having to do anything you don't want to do. Of course, if this is your only definition of freedom, it will feel like a luxury you cannot afford. But what does it look like for us to free our own imaginations, and to free the way we even *think* about freedom? If your understanding of freedom is not bound within the societal systems of oppression and supremacy, what could be possible? If your understanding of freedom is not limited within the worldview of your armor, what else could be true? How do we expand our view of what it means for us to be free?

The idea we are most comfortable with states that if your external world changes—if things change politically, societally, relationally, financially—then you will be free. In this way, your freedom is solely dependent on what the external world chooses to do or not do. Now, I am a fan of living in reality—or at least trying as often as possible to return to reality when I've left it. So I recognize that we do have to engage with systems and circumstances outside of ourselves. This is a huge part of our work to dismantle unjust systems, unlearn their indoctrination, and create liberation for ourselves and for the entire planet. However, we tend to stop there because we think that this is the extent of our fight for freedom and liberation. I would like to invite you to consider that the freedom and liberation you work so hard to create out there starts within you too.

Often when we're using our radical imagination to envision a liberated future, we're thinking about how we can eradicate the problems of external systems and create thriving for the whole community. But what about *you*? Where is your relationship with yourself in that liberated future? How has it shifted, changed, become freer? Is your relationship to yourself liberated, or are you waiting on the world to become just and good sometime in the future before you experience liberation within yourself? Are you a safe space for you? Can you lower your armor when it's just you? Are you able to discern when you're in the middle of the war and you need your armor, or do you carry the war with you everywhere and stay armored up, even when you're alone?

I believe that freedom is a practice, not a state of utopia. We can practice freedom every day, a concept I learned from Ebonyjanice Moore. Our types in nine different ways work hard to keep us safe from harm and in doing so create these safe little boxes for us to live in. We all have different understandings of safety and the behaviors that keep us safe. Freedom, on the other hand, requires us to relax and release some of these behaviors.

Often, the things we do to keep ourselves safe are the opposite of what we need to do to be free. Freedom requires risk, and our singular stories about safety can keep us confined in a sterile box, which is not the same as being free. We don't have to throw out the things that help us feel safe, but we do need to expand our understanding of what is possible outside of our box of perceived safety. As my mother tells me often, there is no safe place for us on earth. So while absolute safety might be impossible, we can build our awareness of what it looks like to be safe *enough*. Safe enough leaves room for risk, and freedom often requires us to take some risks.

- *What does safety mean to you? How do you know when you're safe? Is it a feeling/location/person/intuition?*
- *What are your survival strategies? What behaviors do you engage in to keep yourself safe?*
- *In what ways could your survival strategies be restricting your access to freedom?*
- *What does it look like to be safe enough?*
- *Is it possible for you to honor your need for safety while also leaning into the risk that freedom requires?*

In a video interview with StyleLikeU, Janaya Future Khan says, "If I am to be jailed within the limits of your imagination, you have to remain there as the guard. I am free." In that portion of the interview, Khan was referring to the limited imaginations of the people who actively and consciously choose to uphold systems of supremacy. But I believe that for all of us, our individual and collective imagination of what it looks like to be free has become so limited by the systems we exist within, we've unknowingly become our own internal prison guards.

We spend so much time trying to convince the external world that we don't actually deserve to be locked up in these metaphorical and literal jails, that we are actually free. Meanwhile, we are often the prison guards internally and with each other. All the energy and effort expended in convincing others that we are not how they see us still requires us to remain bound up in proving rather than being. Waiting for them to agree with us, as if they hold the key to the cell, or as if their decision is what creates our freedom.

Recognizing the ways in which we limit our own imagination, the ways in which we hand over our power by waiting for others to validate our freedom first, the ways in which we carry the war with us everywhere we go and stay armored up even when we could be at rest—that's a first step toward embodying some freedom. Sometimes it feels easier to stay in familiar bondage than to actually allow ourselves to be free. The limited box that we live in might be more comfortable than the potential for what freedom could bring. It is important to bring conscious awareness to the ways we limit ourselves so that we can choose something different.

The Risks of Freedom

- *How is your imagination of freedom limited?*
- *Who/what created the limits to your imagination of freedom?*
- *What feels risky about freedom for you?*
- *Where are the places in your life that require you to shift or change in order for you to fully be who you are?*
- *What risks would you need to be willing to take in order to be free?*

Freedom is risky. It's why we try to restrict the abundant freedom of little children. We tell them, "The world isn't safe enough for you to be this free; you have to be quieter/

louder, smaller/bigger, more obedient, less curious to survive." We are taught to limit our inherent fullness to stay safe.

Although these stories we carry with us were formed from our experiences with the external world, our healing requires us to take responsibility for discovering who we are outside of those stories. It began with them saying, "You're only good or loved or safe if X is true." But now, years later, we're still internally telling ourselves those same stories but calling it "reality." There might always be people externally who require us to show up a certain way, but what if we commit to being people who allow ourselves to be fully free in our own relationship to self?

One of the ways we can practice that is by showing up for our young selves and offering the nurture and care they needed but didn't get. You might feel like too much time has passed and that there's no point revisiting the past. But until we actually heal and release, the past is always showing up in the present, whether or not we are conscious of it. Most of the time, we're reacting to the present based on our experiences in the past—good or bad. So it is useful and powerful to go back and hold with care the little version of you that didn't get what they needed, so that the adult you can have access to a more expansive story.

Nurturing Your Inner Child

- *Visualize yourself around the age when you started to learn you had to show up a certain kind of way to be acceptable or survive.*

o *What messages did that version of you need to hear back then? What actions would have helped you feel protected, supported, comforted, seen, nurtured?*

o *Pick one of those messages or actions and offer that in this moment to little you.*

o *Notice what shifts. Maybe there's a shift in your breath or your body's posture. Maybe some emotions arise. Maybe there's more words that come that you want to say to your little self. Honor what arises in the moment as an invitation into your own healing.*

o *Do this practice often. Hold your young self with consideration and kindness, ask them what they need, ask them what they would like to spend their time doing and make space for it. In doing so, you are offering to them a spacious, truer, and more liberated story of who they get to be. Notice how it sets you both free, little by little.*

Knowing that there are risks to freedom can keep us from choosing freedom. We know that for us to be free, certain things must change. The way we talk to ourselves, the way we relate to others outside of ourselves, the way we show up in the world—all of these things might need shifting and changing in order for us to access more freedom. We've heard it said before that freedom isn't actually free. It can cost us our relationships with people who don't want to be close to the freer version of us. They may only want to be close to the version of us that benefits them. Sometimes, freedom means that we have to be okay with disappointing people, with asking for help, with being vulnerable. We have to be okay with not having all the answers or making mistakes. This is a practice. It takes consistent practice to remember that freedom requires risk and to remember what exactly is worth the risk: **YOU**. You are worth the risk. Your freedom and wholeness and full thriving is worth the risk. But you have to be willing to engage in the work it takes to be free.

This isn't flashy or quick work. This is slow work, work that happens a little bit at a time each day. Unlearning our limiting beliefs, creating a different relationship with our imagination around freedom, allowing ourselves to access ease—all of these things are slow work. They require us to show up each day, to practice little freedoms every day. You won't unlearn decades of survival strategy or limiting beliefs in one month or even in one year. But you *can* practice daily one way that you allow yourself to be free. You can continue to build awareness of your limiting beliefs and your limited imagination around freedom and then expand it a little at a time. Taking one step in the direction of freedom will eventually become such a part of the way that you show up with yourself that, over time, you will find that you become freer with yourself.

What limiting beliefs would you need to let go of in order to be free?

1. *I am good and worthy of belonging only when I do everything right and avoid mistakes.*

2. *I am helpful and deserving of love only when I spend all my energy taking care of others and avoiding my own needs.*
3. *I am successful and deserving of love only when I stay busy and productive and avoid failing.*
4. *I am exceptional and deserving of love only when I stand out and avoid being ordinary.*
5. *I am self-sufficient and safe only when I limit my need for others and avoid being incompetent.*
6. *I am vigilant and safe only when I am focused on what could go wrong and avoid uncertainty.*
7. *I am optimistic and safe only when I am focused on opportunities and pleasure and avoid limits and pain.*
8. *I am strong and worthy of belonging only when I am in control and avoid showing vulnerability or weakness.*
9. *I am adaptable and worthy of belonging only when I keep things comfortable and avoid conflict.*

Freedom is not theoretical. It doesn't just live in your mind as a concept. Freedom resides in our cells, in our bodies, and in our lived experiences. We say that we believe in the liberation of all people and everyone's access to freedom, and at the same time, we are regularly unable to have a free relationship with our own bodies or look at people or food or clothes in a way that is free. So the invitation that I am reiterating is that the liberation we believe in and work for "out there" starts within. We have to bring awareness to the places in which we are still bound—in our beliefs and imagination—and offer ourselves a practice of freedom that helps us be more fully who we are, that is to say, more fully free.

What are the little freedoms you can practice every day? Here's a very short list of suggestions to get you started:

- *Make a list of things that bring you joy. Pin that list on your fridge or somewhere you can see it regularly. Make time to do one thing off that list each day.*
- *Similarly, make a list of things your childhood self enjoyed doing. Make time for play as a way to nurture your inner child.*
- *To combat self-criticism, make a practice of noticing what is good enough about you each day.*
- *Ask for help with the little things too. You don't need to wait until you're overwhelmed.*
- *Say no more often. Set and honor the boundaries that help you thrive.*
- *Slow down. Practice being present when you eat or drink, when you're in conversations, when you're on a walk, etc. Bringing your full attention to the present moment allows for a deeper experience of pleasure, satisfaction, and balance.*
- *Discover what "enough" feels like in your body. Enough water, rest, food, touch, money, time, etc. Learn how to be satisfiable so you can free yourself from capitalism's insatiable drive for excess.*

- *Don't ignore your feelings. Pay attention to where your body is holding anger, fear, sadness, and joy each day. Feel and release.*
- *Let a trusted person (or people) see the vulnerable parts of you. Allow yourself to feel the ease of not having to hide or deny in those moments. Let yourself be cared for.*
- *If, for a moment, you set aside your ideal self— the you who has to be right, helpful, successful, unique, self-sufficient, vigilant, optimistic, strong, and adaptable—what else is good about you? What else do you like about you? Create more space for those parts.*
- *Become friends with the parts of yourself you habitually avoid—your messiness, needs, failures, ordinariness, incompetence, uncertainty, limitations, weaknesses, and anger.*
  - o *When you notice these things in yourself, instead of being the prison guard and shaming yourself back into compliance, try something new. Withhold criticism or judgment and just allow that part to be there.*
  - o *Notice what story you tell yourself about what it means to allow this part of you to exist. What if that story wasn't always true?*
  - o *Offer kindness just like you did with your inner child. Notice what shifts in your heart and body.*

Finally, I want to emphasize that freedom is not escapism. These prompts and practices are to help us find an inner freedom and spaciousness around our limiting beliefs *while* we navigate the very real external threats to the well-being of people across the globe. Practicing these little freedoms allows us to be more resourced and grounded as we continue to engage in our work. It helps us stop policing ourselves internally, which then reduces how often we police each other externally.

A greater experience of internal freedom does not mean we check out of reality. In fact, the more space we create around these limiting stories that keep us fundamentally isolated from each other, the deeper our awareness grows of our interconnectedness and interdependence. So if you find that you are using these practices as a way to feel superior and separate from others, you're doing it wrong. If you find that the more internal freedom you experience, the deeper your active compassion grows for all of humanity, then keep going.

NOTES

Chapter 1

The Black woman is the mule of the world: Zora Neale Hurston, *Their Eyes Were Watching God* (1937; repr., New York: HarperLuxe, 2008), 21.

The function of freedom: Toni Morrison, "Cinderella's Stepsisters," in *The Source of Self-Regard: Selected Essays, Speeches, and Meditations* (New York: Alfred A. Knopf, 2019), 111.

Renée Rosario, The Narrative Enneagram's Enneagram Intensive 2.0 (lecture, Vallombrosa Center, Menlo Park, CA, July 30, 2017).

Tricia Hersey, our collective Nap Bishop: The Nap Ministry (website), accessed June 28, 2021, https://thenapministry.wordpress.com/.

Chapter 2

In one of my favorite quotes: Stephen R. Covey, A. Roger Merrill, and Rebecca R. Merrill, *First Things First* (1994; repr., New York: Free Press, 2003), 59.

Chapter 3

Power, in social justice work: Antoinette Myers and Yuka Ogino, *Power, Privilege, & Oppression* (PowerPoint presentation, Scripps College, Claremont, CA), https://tinyurl.com/438twu6r.

Power within is the capacity to imagine: Lisa VeneKlasen et al., "Power and Empowerment," chap. 3 in *A New Weave of Power, People, & Politics: The Action Guide for Advocacy and Citizen Participation* (Oklahoma City, OK: World Neighbors, 2002), 45, https://tinyurl.com/3dtf6kck.

Refers to our collective power: VeneKlasen et al., 45.

What Andre Henry was illustrating: Andre Henry (@theandrehenry), "This 2 minutes reveals a lesson about power that changed my life forever," Facebook video, January 21, 2020, https://tinyurl.com/3662pswb; Andre Henry, "We Need a Spectacular Intervention," (Pasadena, CA: All Saints Church, January 19, 2020), video shared by All

Saints Church Pasadena, January 19, 2020, on YouTube, 19:07, https://tinyurl.com/48mmcwms.
Some have "reduced capacity": Catriona Mackenzie, Wendy Rogers, and Susan Dodds, "Introduction: What Is Vulnerability and Why Does It Matter for Moral Theory?," in *Vulnerability: New Essays in Ethics and Feminist Philosophy*, ed. Mackenzie, Rogers, and Dodds (New York: Oxford University Press, 2014), 6.

Chapter 5

Our bodies take in eleven million bits: Emily Kwong, "Understanding Unconscious Bias," interview with Pragya Agarwal, July 15, 2020 on NPR, *Short Wave*, produced by Rebecca Ramirez, https://tinyurl.com/4mswymv6.

Chapter 8

The prayer: Alcoholics Anonymous, *Twelve Steps and Twelve Traditions*, 40th printing (New York: Alcoholics Anonymous World Services, 2004), 41.

Chapter 16

One of my favorite Mary Oliver poems: Mary Oliver, "*Messenger,*" in *Thirst* (Boston: Beacon Press, 2006), 1.

A Guide to Practicing Freedom

In a video interview with: Janaya Future Kahn, "Non-Binary Activist Janaya Khan is the Future's Brightest Light," interview by StyleLike, February 4, 2021, https://www.youtube.com/watch?app=desktop&v 7vmpxcq_XZg.